PROCESSING BOOKKEEPING TRANSACTIONS

Qualifications and Credit Framework

AQ2013 Level 2 Certificate in Accounting

British Library Cataloguing-in-Publication Data

A catalogue record for this book is available from the British Library.

Published by
Kaplan Publishing UK
Unit 2, The Business Centre
Molly Millars Lane
Wokingham
Berkshire
RG41 2QZ

ISBN: 978-0-85732-862-5

The text in this material and any others made available by any Kaplan Group company does not amount to advice on a particular matter and should not be taken as such. No reliance should be placed on the content as the basis for any investment or other decision or in connection with any advice given to third parties. Please consult your appropriate professional adviser as necessary. Kaplan Publishing Limited and all other Kaplan group companies expressly disclaim all liability to any person in respect of any losses or other claims, whether direct, indirect, incidental, consequential or otherwise arising in relation to the use of such materials.

Printed and bound in Great Britain.

We are grateful to the Association of Accounting Technicians for permission to reproduce past assessment materials and example tasks based on the new syllabus. The solutions to past assessments and similar activities in the style of the new syllabus have been prepared by Kaplan Publishing.

CONTENTS

KAPLAN PUBLISHING

INTRODUCTION

HOW TO USE THESE MATERIALS

These Kaplan Publishing learning materials have been carefully designed to make your learning experience as easy as possible and to give you the best chance of success in your AAT assessments.

They contain a number of features to help you in the study process.

The sections on the Unit Guide, the Assessment and Study Skills should be read before you commence your studies.

They are designed to familiarise you with the nature and content of the assessment and to give you tips on how best to approach your studies.

STUDY TEXT

This study text has been specially prepared for the revised AAT qualification introduced in September 2013.

It is written in a practical and interactive style:

- key terms and concepts are clearly defined

- all topics are illustrated with practical examples with clearly worked solutions based on sample tasks provided by the AAT in the new assessment style

- frequent activities throughout the chapters ensure that what you have learnt is regularly reinforced

- 'pitfalls' and 'examination tips' help you avoid commonly made mistakes and help you focus on what is required to perform well in your assessment

- practice workbook activities can be completed at the end of each chapter.

WORKBOOK

The workbook comprises:

Practice activities at the end of each chapter with solutions at the end of the text, to reinforce the work covered in each chapter.

The questions are divided into their relevant chapters and students may either attempt these questions as they work through the textbook, or leave some or all of these until they have completed the textbook as a final revision of what they have studied.

ICONS

The study chapters include the following icons throughout.

They are designed to assist you in your studies by identifying key definitions and the points at which you can test yourself on the knowledge gained.

Definition

These sections explain important areas of Knowledge which must be understood and reproduced in an assessment

Example

The illustrative examples can be used to help develop an understanding of topics before attempting the activity exercises

Activity

These are exercises which give the opportunity to assess your understanding of all the assessment areas.

Quality and accuracy are of the upmost importance to us so if you spot an error in any of our products, please send an email to mykaplanreporting@kaplan.com with full details, or follow the link to the feedback form in MyKaplan.

Our Quality Co-ordinator will work with our technical team to verify the error and take action to ensure it is corrected in future editions.

UNIT GUIDE

Processing Bookkeeping Transactions is the first of two financial accounting assessments at level 2.

Purpose of the units

The AAT has stated that this unit will enable the student to develop an understanding of a manual double entry bookkeeping system to the initial trial balance stage.

Students will develop the necessary knowledge and skills to deal with documents that are sent to and from organisations. They will need to know how to make entries in sales, purchases and returns day books using account codes, and to transfer those totals to the sales, purchases and general ledgers. The cash-book and petty cash-book are also dealt with in this unit, making entries into both and transferring totals to the ledgers.

Students will learn how to make appropriate checks on supplier invoices and credit notes, reconcile supplier statements with the purchases ledger account and calculate payments due to suppliers. They will also learn how to prepare sales invoices and credit notes and check receipts from customers.

Learning objectives

On completion of these units the learner will be able to:

- Understand the principles of processing financial transactions.
- Understand the double entry bookkeeping system.
- Understand discounts.
- Prepare and process the financial documentation for customers.
- Process supplier invoices and credit notes and calculate payments.
- Maintain the cash-book.
- Maintain petty cash records.
- Process ledger transactions and extract a trial balance.

Learning Outcomes and Assessment criteria

The unit consists of eight learning outcomes. These are set out in the following table with Learning Outcomes in bold type and Assessment criteria listed underneath each Learning Outcome. Reference is also made to the relevant chapter within the text.

Knowledge

To perform this unit effectively you will need to know and understand the following:

		Chapter
1	**Understand the principles of processing financial transactions**	
1.1	Outline the purpose and content of these business documents • petty cash voucher • invoice • credit note • remittance advice • statement of account	1, 8
1.2	Explain the purpose and content of the books of prime entry	2
1.3	List the ways in which customers may pay an organisation and an organisation may pay its suppliers	8
2	**Understand the double entry bookkeeping system**	
2.1	Explain the accounting equation and how it relates to a double entry bookkeeping system	3
2.2	Outline how the books of prime entry integrate with the double entry bookkeeping system	2
2.3	Describe the function of a coding system within a double entry bookkeeping system	1

KAPLAN PUBLISHING

		Chapter
2.4	Describe the processing of financial transactions from the books of prime entry into the double entry bookkeeping system	7
2.5	Define capital income and capital expenditure	3
2.6	Define revenue income and revenue expenditure	3
3	**Understand discounts**	
3.1	Explain the difference between settlement, trade and bulk discount	1, 5
3.2	Describe the effect that a settlement discount has on the sales tax (e.g. VAT) charged	5, 6

Skills

To perform this unit effectively you will need to be able to do the following.

		Chapter
4	**Prepare and process financial documentation for customers**	
4.1	Use source documents to prepare invoices or credit notes	1, 5
4.2	Calculate invoice or credit note amounts reflecting any:	5, 6
	• Trade discount	
	• Bulk discount	
	• Settlement discount	
	• Sales tax (VAT)	
4.3	Enter sales invoices and credit notes into books of prime entry using suitable codes	2
4.4	Check the accuracy of receipts from customers against relevant supporting documentation	8
4.5	Produce statements of account to send to credit customers	8

KAPLAN PUBLISHING

THE ASSESSMENT

The format of the assessment

The assessment contains ten tasks in one section.

Students will normally be assessed by computer-based assessment and will be required to respond to CBT tasks in a variety of ways, for example using multiple choice, true/false, drag and drop, drop-down lists, text select, linking boxes, gap fill tools and AAT purpose built question types to reflect real workplace activities.

Task	Maximum marks	Title for topics within task range
1	15	Make entries in an analysed day book
2	15	Transfer data from day books to ledgers
3	20	Make entries in a three column cash book
4	15	Transfer data from a three column cash book
5	20	Make entries in and transfers from an analysed petty cash book
6	20	Prepare an initial trial balance
7	15	Check supplier invoices/credit notes
8	15	Prepare sales invoice or credit note
		Check the accuracy of receipts from customers
9	15	Prepare a statement of account from an account in the sales ledger
10	15	Understand the double entry bookkeeping system

Time allowed

The time allowed for this assessment is **two hours.**

Terminology

Students should be familiar with IFRS terminology. Other terms are used in this document to match titles provided by the QCF.

STUDY SKILLS

Preparing to study

Devise a study plan

Determine which times of the week you will study.

Split these times into sessions of at least one hour for study of new material. Any shorter periods could be used for revision or practice.

Put the times you plan to study onto a study plan for the weeks from now until the assessment and set yourself targets for each period of study – in your sessions make sure you cover the whole course, activities and the associated questions with answers at the back of the Study Text.

If you are studying more than one unit at a time, try to vary your subjects as this can help to keep you interested and see subjects as part of wider knowledge.

When working through your course, compare your progress with your plan and, if necessary, re-plan your work (perhaps including extra sessions) or, if you are ahead, do some extra revision/practice questions.

Effective studying

Active reading

You are not expected to learn the text by rote, rather, you must understand what you are reading and be able to use it to pass the assessment and develop good practice.

A good technique is to use SQ3Rs – Survey, Question, Read, Recall, Review:

1   Survey the chapter

Look at the headings and read the introduction, knowledge, skills and content, so as to get an overview of what the chapter deals with.

2   Question

Whilst undertaking the survey ask yourself the questions you hope the chapter will answer for you.

3   Read

Read through the chapter thoroughly working through the activities and, at the end, making sure that you can meet the learning objectives shown within the summary.

4   Recall

At the end of each section and at the end of the chapter, try to recall the main ideas of the section/chapter without referring to the text. This is best done after short break of a couple of minutes after the reading stage.

5   Review

Check that your recall notes are correct.

You may also find it helpful to re-read the chapter to try and see the topic(s) it deals with as a whole.

Note taking

Taking notes is a useful way of learning, but do not simply copy out the text.

The notes must:

- be in your own words
- be concise
- cover the key points
- be well organised
- be modified as you study further chapters in this text or in related ones.

Trying to summarise a chapter without referring to the text can be a useful way of determining which areas you know and which you don't.

Three ways of taking notes

1   Summarise the key points of a chapter

2   Make linear notes

A list of headings, subdivided with sub-headings listing the key points.

If you use linear notes, you can use different colours to highlight key points and keep topic areas together.

Use plenty of space to make your notes easy to use.

3   Try a diagrammatic form

The most common of which is a mind map.

To make a mind map, put the main heading in the centre of the paper and put a circle around it.

Draw lines radiating from this to the main sub-headings which again have circles around them.

Continue the process from the sub-headings to sub-sub-headings.

Highlighting and underlining

You may find it useful to underline or highlight key points in your study text – but do be selective.

You may also wish to make notes in the margins.

Revision phase

Kaplan has produced material specifically designed for your final assessment preparation for this unit.

These include pocket revision notes and a bank of revision questions specifically in the style of the new syllabus.
Further guidance on how to approach the final stage of your studies is given in these materials.

Further reading

In addition to this text, you should also read the 'Student section' of the 'Accounting Technician' magazine every month to keep abreast of any guidance from the examiners.

Business documents

1

Introduction

The purpose of accounting is to record and classify business transactions. There are many transactions that a business may undertake; credit sales, credit purchases, cash sales, cash purchases, other expenses either paid from the bank or by cash, paying cash into the bank, withdrawing cash from the bank and owner's drawings.

Various documents may be used when dealing with business transactions. This chapter reviews the flow of a transaction including the documents involved.

The name of a transaction or document will depend on whether we are looking at it from the point of view of the seller or the purchaser. Thus an invoice may be called a 'sales invoice' for the seller but a 'purchase invoice' for the purchaser, it is the same invoice. Similarly, the seller makes a 'sale' and the purchaser makes a 'purchase', it is the same transaction.

KNOWLEDGE	CONTENTS
Outline the purpose and content of a range of business documents to include (1.1) – Invoice – Credit note Describe the function of a coding system within a double entry bookkeeping system (2.3) Explain the difference between settlement, trade and bulk discount (3.1)	1 Cash vs credit 2 Summary of the flow of documents 3 Quotation 4 Purchase order 5 Sales order 6 Delivery note 7 Invoice 8 Operation of VAT 9 Discounts 10 Preparing an invoice 11 Credit note 12 Coding

SKILLS

Use source documents to prepare invoices or credit notes (4.1)

Check accuracy of supplier invoices and credit notes against these source documents (5.1)

–   Purchase orders

–   Goods received notes

–   Delivery notes

1 Cash vs credit

1.1 Introduction

Cash sales and purchases are relatively straightforward but credit sales and purchases are more involved. Dependent on whether we are the seller or the buyer dictates whether we view the transaction as a sale or purchase. The details of all of the aspects covered here will be dealt with in greater depth in later chapters.

1.2 Cash sales and purchases

A cash sale or purchase will normally be made in a retail environment. A customer will enter the shop, choose the goods they wish to buy then come to the till in order to pay for them. The seller will tell the customer the price of the goods and the customer then offers payment for them, in the form of notes and coins. Alternatively, the customer may offer to pay for the goods by debit card, cheque or credit card.

Finally, once the customer has paid for the goods, a receipt of some sort will be given to the customer. This may be printed automatically by the till or may be a handwritten receipt in some businesses. The transaction is now complete.

1.3 Credit sales and purchases

The procedure for a sale or purchase on credit can be rather more involved. The sale or purchase process will normally be initiated by a seller receiving an order from a customer. This order may be in writing, by fax, over the telephone or by email. When your business receives the order, the first decision that must be made is whether or not to allow the customer credit for this sale i.e. a period of time they can take before paying the invoice.

1.4 Offering credit

Selling goods on credit always involves an element of risk. The goods are being taken away or delivered to the customer now with the promise of payment in the future. Therefore your business must be confident that the payment will be received. The decision process as to whether or not to make the sale on credit will be different depending upon whether this is a sale to an existing credit customer or a new customer.

1.5 Existing customers

If an existing credit customer wishes to make a further purchase on credit, it would be normal practice to carry out some basic checks. When the customer was originally taken on as a credit customer, a credit limit will have been set which should not be exceeded. Checks should be made to ensure that the new sale, when added to the amount currently owing, do not take the customer over their credit limit.

It would also be sensible to check that there have been no problems recently with receiving payment from this customer. If the checks are satisfactory then the credit sale can go ahead.

1.6 New customer

If a new customer asks for credit from your business then it would be normal practice to ask the customer to supply some trade references – names of other businesses that they trade with on credit who can vouch for their creditworthiness. Your business may also wish to check the customer's creditworthiness through an agency, or by asking for references from the customer's bank.

If the references and checks are satisfactory then a credit limit will be set for this customer and the sale can go ahead.

---

2 Summary of the flow of documents

The main document flows for a credit transaction are illustrated below. The various documents are described in the paragraphs that follow.

SELLER		CUSTOMER
Price Quotation →		
←	Purchase Order	
Sales Order →		
Delivery Note	+ Goods →	
Sales Invoice →		
Credit Note →		
←	Cheque	

3.1 Price enquiry

The first stage of the process of a credit sale may be the receipt of a price enquiry from a customer.

The price enquiry may be a formal written document, an email enquiry or more likely a telephone call. When responding to a price enquiry it is important that you make sure that the price you quote is the correct one as if it is incorrect you may find that you are contracted to sell the goods at that price under contract law.

3.2 Price quotation

In some organisations it is common practice to quote prices to customers over the telephone particularly if there is a catalogue or price list from which there are no deviations in price. However, some businesses will be prepared to offer certain customers goods at different prices. Therefore it is often the case that a price quotation is sent out to a customer showing the price at which the goods that they want can be bought.

There may also be discounts offered and/or given to customers which we will consider later.

A typical price quotation is shown on the next page.

City Woods Suppliers

192 Old Kent Road
London
SE1 8QT

*Name and address of
business quoting price*

Tel: 020 7248 7009 – Fax: 020 728 7890

QUOTATION

TO: Alpha Limited
Mountjoy Street
London W12 6RS

*Name and address of
customer*

Date: 14 Sept 20X3

Today's date

Thank you for your telephone enquiry of 10 September. We are pleased to quote the following price:

Chipboard sheeting 6' × 4' Code CB0351 £23.00 per unit, excluding VAT

*Details of
goods*

*Price being
quoted*

J Kramer

*Authorisation
signature*

Sales Manager

The price quotation is an important document as this is the price that your organisation is now contracted to sell the goods at. Therefore it is important that it is authorised by the appropriate person in the organisation.

4 Purchase order

4.1 The purchase order

If the customer is happy with the price quotation that they have received from your business then they will place a firm order with you. The order may be by telephone or it may be in writing. Whatever method is used for the purchase order, it is important to check all of the details carefully.

- Does the price agree to what was quoted to the customer?

- Are the delivery terms acceptable?

- Are any discounts applicable?

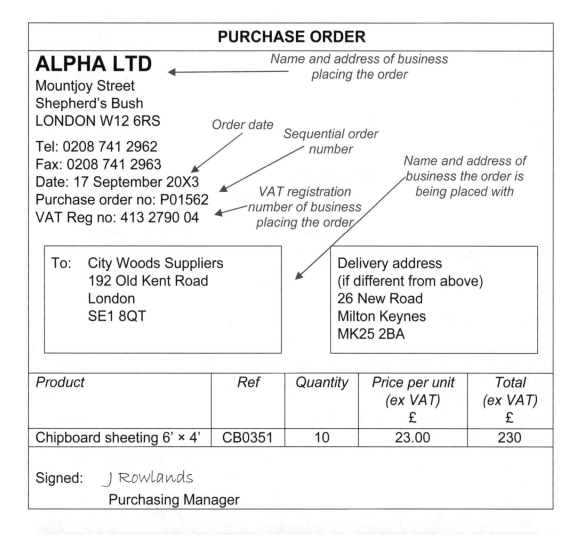

PURCHASE ORDER

ALPHA LTD ← *Name and address of business placing the order*

Mountjoy Street
Shepherd's Bush
LONDON W12 6RS

Tel: 0208 741 2962
Fax: 0208 741 2963
Date: 17 September 20X3
Purchase order no: P01562
VAT Reg no: 413 2790 04

Order date
Sequential order number
Name and address of business the order is being placed with
VAT registration number of business placing the order

| To: | City Woods Suppliers 192 Old Kent Road London SE1 8QT | | Delivery address (if different from above) 26 New Road Milton Keynes MK25 2BA |

Product	Ref	Quantity	Price per unit (ex VAT) £	Total (ex VAT) £
Chipboard sheeting 6' × 4'	CB0351	10	23.00	230

Signed: *J Rowlands*
Purchasing Manager

5 Sales order

5.1 Confirming sales orders

To avoid misunderstandings, a supplier will normally confirm a customer's order by completing a **sales order**, even if the customer has already sent a written purchase order.

A **sales order** is a document confirming:

- quantity/type of goods or service
- date of supply
- location of supply
- price and terms.

City Woods Suppliers

192 Old Kent Road
London
SE1 8QT

*Name and address
of business making
the sale*

*Delivery address
and date*

Tel: 020 7248 7009 – Fax: 020 7248 7890

SALES ORDER

To:

Alpha Limited
Mountjoy St
London W12 6RS

*Name and
address of
customer*

Delivery:

26 New Road
Milton Keynes
MK25 2BA

Delivery date:

25 September 20X3

*Sales order
number*

Date: 20 September 20X3

Sales order number: 41161

We confirm the following order to be delivered as above.
Please note our credit terms are strictly 30 days net.

Code	Quantity	Description	Unit price (excl VAT)	Discount
CB0351	10	Chipboard sheeting 6' × 4'	£23.00	NIL

Details of goods

Price of goods

*Authorised
signature*

Authorised: *P. Anders*   Date: 20 September 20X3

6 Delivery note

6.1 Introduction

Once all of the negotiations over the price and terms of the credit sale have been completed, then the goods themselves must be delivered.

6.2 Delivery notes

Delivery note – a document accompanying goods despatched to a customer.

Delivery notes should have **sequential numbers** that are either pre-printed for a manual system or computer generated in a computer system, and should be used in order. Spoiled delivery notes should be cancelled and kept.

There will normally be three parts to a delivery note:

Part one – This is kept by the **customer** in order to compare to the purchase order and then to the sales invoice

Part two – This is signed and returned to the **supplier** of the goods as evidence that they have been received by the customer in good condition.

Part three – This is signed and kept by the **delivery organisation** as evidence that they have delivered the goods and that the customer has received them.

City Woods Suppliers

192 Old Kent Road
London
SE1 8QT

Tel: 020 7248 7009 – Fax: 020 7248 7890   DN 005673

DELIVERY NOTE

To:	**Delivery:**	**Delivery date:**
Alpha Limited	26 New Road	25 September 20X3
Mountjoy St	Milton Keynes	
London W12 6RS	MK25 2BA	
Date: 25 September 20X3		**Sales order number:** 41161

We confirm the following order to be delivered as above.

Product	Code	Quantity
Chipboard 6' × 4'	CB0351	10

Received in good condition: *A Patel*

---

7 Invoice

7.1 The sales invoice

Once the goods have been delivered the seller must prepare and send out the sales invoice.

In a manual system, sales invoices must be prepared from the details shown on delivery notes. Delivery notes do not normally show details of prices, discounts or VAT. (This is because the customer might mistake the delivery note for a sales invoice.) Price, discounts and VAT are shown on the sales invoice.

Sales invoices should have pre-printed sequential numbers and should be used in order. Spoiled sales invoices should be cancelled and kept.

In a computer system, the sales invoice will generally be produced at the same time as the delivery note and will be identical except that the delivery note may not have details of price, etc.

City Woods Suppliers

192 Old Kent Road
London
SE1 8QT

Tel: 020 7248 7009 – Fax: 020 7248 7890

Invoice no:	1005673
Tax point:	25 September 20X3
VAT reg no:	618 2201 63
Delivery note:	DN005673
Account no:	AL6215

INVOICE

To:
Alpha Limited
Mountjoy St
London W12 6RS

Delivery:
26 New Road
Milton Keynes
MK25 2BA

Delivery date:
25 September 20X3

Date: 25 September 20X3   **Sales order number:** 41161

We confirm the following order to be delivered as above.

Product	Code	Quantity	Price per unit £	Total £
Chipboard 6' × 4'	CB0351	10	23.00	230.00
			VAT	46.00
			Total	276.00

7.2   Pricing goods and services

Unit prices for goods or services are kept in master files which must be updated regularly. If a price quotation has been sent to a customer then this must be used to determine the price to use on the invoice.

Prices will normally be quoted exclusive of value added tax (VAT), as this is the true selling price to the business.

8   Operation of VAT

8.1   Introduction

Sales tax (VAT) is a tax levied on **consumer** expenditure. However the procedure is that it is collected at each stage in the production and distribution chain. Most businesses (being **taxable persons** as defined later) avoid having to treat VAT as an expense as they may deduct the VAT they have paid on their purchases **(input tax)** from the VAT they charge to customers on their sales **(output tax)** and pay only the difference to the tax authorities (HM Revenue and Customs).

8.2   How VAT works

Let us examine a simple illustration. We will assume a standard rate of 20%, and follow one article, a wooden table, through the production and distribution chain.

- A private individual cuts down a tree and sells it to a timber mill for £10. **Tax effect** – none. The individual is not a 'taxable person' in this case.

- The timber mill saws the log and sells the timber to a furniture manufacturer for £100 + VAT.

   Tax effect – Being a taxable person, the mill is obliged to charge its customers VAT at 20% on the selling price (output tax).There is no input tax available for offset.

   Cash effect – The mill collected £120 from the customer (or has a receivable for this sum). Of this, £20 has to be paid to HMRC and therefore only £100 would be recognised as sales.

- The manufacturer makes a table from the wood, and sells this to a retailer for £400 + VAT.

  Tax effect – The manufacturer is obliged to charge VAT at 20% on the selling price (i.e. £80), but in this instance would be allowed to reduce this amount by setting off the input tax of £20 charged on the purchase of wood from the mill.

  Cash effect – Tax of £60 is paid to the tax authorities (HM Revenue and Customs) (output less input tax = £80 less £20). £400 is recognised as sales and £100 as purchases in the accounts.

- The retailer sells the table to a private customer for £1,000 plus VAT of £200. **Tax effect** – The retailer charges £200 of VAT to the customer but against this output tax may be set off the input tax of £80 charged on the purchase from the manufacturer.

  Cash effect – £120 (£200 – £80) is paid to HMRC. Purchases would be shown in the books at £400 and sales at £1,000.

- **The private customer** – VAT is a tax levied on consumer expenditure and the chain ends here. The customer is not a taxable person, and cannot recover the tax paid.

You will note that everybody else has passed the sales on and, though the customer has paid his £200 to the retailer, HMRC has received its tax by contributions from each link in the chain, as shown below:

	£
Timber mill	20.00
Manufacturer	60.00
Retailer	120.00
	————
	200.00
	————

🔍 Definitions

VAT is charged on the **taxable supply of goods and services** in the United Kingdom by a **taxable person** in the course of a business carried on by him.

Output tax is the tax charged on the sale of goods and services

Input tax is the tax paid on the purchase of goods and services

KAPLAN PUBLISHING

8.3 Taxable supply of goods and services

Taxable supply is the supply of all items except those which are **exempt.** Examples of exempt items are as follows:

- certain land and buildings, where sold, leased or hired

- insurance

- Post Office postal services

- betting, gaming and lotteries.

Input tax cannot be reclaimed where the trader's supplies are all exempt.

8.4 Rates of VAT

In the UK, there are three rates of VAT on taxable supplies. Some items are 'zero-rated' (similar to exempt except that input tax can be reclaimed), there is a special rate of 5% for domestic fuel and power, and all other items are rated at the standard rate of 20%. Examples of 'zero-rated' supplies include:

- water and most types of food

- books and newspapers

- drugs and medicines

- children's clothing and footwear.

8.5 Non-deductible VAT

VAT on some items is non-deductible. This means that VAT on any purchases of these items cannot be deducted from the amount of tax payable to HMRC. The business has to bear the VAT as an expense.

Non-deductible items include:

- motor cars

- business entertaining.

For our purposes you will normally be dealing with taxable supplies at the standard rate of 20%.

8.6 Taxable person

A taxable person is any individual, partnership, company, etc who intends to make taxable supplies and is liable to register.

A person is liable to register if the value of his taxable supplies exceeds a specified amount in a 12-month period. Most companies and partnerships and many sole traders are liable to register.

8.7 VAT exclusive amounts

If you are given the net price of goods, the price excluding VAT, then the amount of VAT is 20/100 of this price.

Note: VAT is always rounded down to the nearest penny.

Example

A sale is made for £360.48 plus VAT. What is the amount of VAT to be charged on this sale?

Solution

VAT = £360.48 × 20/100 = £72.09

Remember to round down to the nearest penny.

An alternative way of calculating this would to be to multiply the net amount of £360.48 by 20%:

VAT = £360.48 × 20% = £72.09

8.8 VAT inclusive amounts

If a price is given that already includes the VAT then calculating the VAT requires an understanding of the price structure where VAT is concerned.

	%
Selling price incl. VAT (gross)	120
VAT	20
	___
Selling price excl. VAT (net)	100
	___

Example

Goods have a selling price of £3,000 inclusive of VAT. What is the VAT on the goods and the net price of these goods?

Solution

	£
Net price (£3,000 × 100/120)	2,500
VAT (£3,000 × 20/120)	500
	___
Gross price	3,000
	___

KAPLAN PUBLISHING

Activity 1

What is the amount of VAT on each of the following transactions?

(i)   £100 net of VAT

(ii) £250 net of VAT

(iii) £480 including VAT

(iv) £600 including VAT

8.9   VAT and discounts

The impact of discounts on VAT calculations will be considered in a later chapter.

9   Discounts

9.1   Trade discounts

Trade discounts are a definite amount that is deducted from the list price of the goods for the supplies to some customers, with the intention of encouraging and rewarding customer loyalty. The actual calculation of the trade discount on the face of the invoice should be checked and it should be agreed that the correct percentage of trade discount has been deducted.

9.2   Bulk discounts

A bulk discount is similar to a trade discount in that it is deducted from the list price on the invoice. However, a bulk discount is given by a supplier for orders above a certain size. As with a trade discount the calculation of any bulk discount must be checked to the agreement between customer and supplier, to ensure that the correct discount has been given.

9.3   Settlement or cash discounts

Settlement or cash discounts are offered to customers in order to encourage early payment of invoices. The details of the settlement discount will normally be shown at the bottom of the invoice and it is up to the customer to decide whether to pay the invoice early enough to benefit from the settlement discount or whether to delay payment and ignore the settlement discount.

The agreement between the customer and supplier should be checked to ensure that the correct percentage of settlement discount according to the correct terms has been offered.

A trade discount or a bulk discount is a definite reduction in price from the list price whereas a cash or settlement discount is only a reduction in price if the organisation decides to take advantage of it by paying earlier.

9.4 VAT calculations and discounts

We will consider the impact on VAT calculations when discounts are offered in a later chapter.

10 Preparing an invoice

10.1 Preparing a sales invoice

In order to prepare the sales invoice the customer master file must be found. This will show the details of any discounts, etc offered to this customer.

 **Example**

Preparing a sales invoice

Thelma Goody is the sales invoicing clerk for a VAT registered clothing wholesaler. Thelma prepares the sales invoices to be sent to the customer from the price list and a copy of the delivery note sent up to her by the sales department.

Today she has received the following delivery note from the sales department.

Delivery note: 2685

To: Kids Clothes Ltd
9 Port Street
MANCHESTER
M1 5EX

A B Fashions Ltd
3 Park Road
Parkway
Bristol
BR6 6SJ
Tel: 01272 695221
Fax: 01272 695222

Delivery date: 20 August 20X6

Quantity	Code	DESCRIPTION	Colour
90	SSB 330	Shawls (babies)	Assorted
30	CJA 991	Cashmere jumpers (adult)	Cream
30	GGC 442	Gloves (children)	Assorted

Received by: ....

Signature: .... Date: ....

Code	Description	Colour	Unit price £	VAT rate
SSG 001	Skirt (girls)	Black	13.50	Zero
SSW 002	Skirt (women)	Navy	15.90	Standard
TTW 037	Trousers (women)	Black	21.00	Standard
TTW 038	Trousers (women)	Navy	15.60	Standard
TTW 039	Trousers (women)	Red	15.60	Standard
SSB 330	Shawl (babies)	Assorted	11.50	Zero
SSB 331	Shawl (babies)	White	11.50	Zero
CJA 991	Cashmere jumper (adult)	Cream	65.00	Standard
CJA 992	Cashmere jumper (adult)	Pink	65.00	Standard
CJA 993	Cashmere jumper (adult)	Blue	65.00	Standard
CJA 994	Cashmere jumper (adult)	Camel	65.00	Standard
HHB 665	Hat (babies)	White	3.50	Zero
HHB 666	Hat (babies)	Blue	3.50	Zero
GGC 442	Gloves (children)	Assorted	6.20	Zero
GGC 443	Gloves (children)	White	6.50	Zero
GGC 444	Gloves (children)	Black	6.50	Zero

The customer file shows that Kids Clothes Ltd's account number is KC 0055 and that a trade discount of 10% is offered to this customer.

Thelma must now prepare the sales invoice. Today's date is 22 August 20X6. The last invoice number was 95123.

Solution

INVOICE

Invoice to:
Kids Clothes Ltd
9 Port Street
MANCHESTER
M1 5EX

A B Fashions Ltd
3 Park Road
Parkway
Bristol
BR6 6SJ
Tel: 01272 695221
Fax: 01272 695222

Deliver to:

As above

Invoice no:	95124
Tax point:	22 August 20X6
VAT reg no:	488 7922 26
Delivery note no:	2685
Account no:	KC 0055

Code	Description	Quantity	VAT rate	Unit price	Amount excl of VAT
			%	£	£
SSB 330	Shawls (babies) assorted	90	0	11.50	1,035.00
CJA 991	Cashmere jumper (adult) cream	30	20	65.00	1,950.00
GGC 442	Gloves (children) assorted	30	0	6.20	186.00
					3,171.00
Trade discount 10%					(317.10)
					2,853.90
VAT					351.00
Total amount payable					3,204.90

Step 1 Enter today's date on the invoice and the invoice number which should be the next number after the last sales invoice number.

Step 2 Enter the customer details – name, address and account number.

Step 3	Refer now to the delivery note copy and enter the delivery note number and the quantities, codes and descriptions of the goods.
Step 4	Refer to the price list and enter the unit prices of the goods and the rate of VAT (note that the VAT rate for children's clothes is zero).
Step 5	Now for the calculations – firstly multiply the number of each item by the unit price to find the VAT exclusive price – then total these total prices – finally calculate the trade discount as 10% of this total, £3,171 × 10% = £317.10 and deduct it.
Step 6	Calculate the VAT – in this case there is only standard rate VAT on the cashmere jumpers but you must remember to deduct the trade discount (£1,950 – £195) before calculating the VAT amount £1,755 × 20% = £351 – add the VAT to the invoice total after deducting the trade discount.

10.2 The purchase invoice

Now considering the perspective of the customer, what we previously have viewed as a sales invoice, to the customer is a purchase invoice. Once the customer receives their purchase invoice from the seller, a number of checks need to be made on it before it can be passed for payment.

10.3 Order and receipt of goods

Firstly the purchase invoice must be checked to the purchase order and to the delivery note. This is to ensure that not only is this an invoice for goods that were ordered but also for goods that were received. In particular check the description and the quantity of the goods.

For example suppose that the purchase order for goods shows that 100 packs were ordered and the delivery note shows that 100 packs were received. If when the invoice arrives it is for 120 packs then the supplier should be politely informed of the error and a credit note requested.

10.4 Calculations

All of the calculations on the invoice should also be checked to ensure that they are correct. This will include the following:

- all pricing calculations
- any trade discount or bulk discount calculations

- the VAT calculations remembering any settlement discounts that may be offered (to be covered in a later chapter)

- the total addition of the invoice.

10.5 Other terms found on invoices

You may also find other terms and conditions shown on invoices or other documents. Here are some of the more common:

E & OE – Errors and omissions excepted. The seller is claiming the right to correct any genuine errors on the invoice (e.g. prices) at a later date.

Carriage paid – The invoice value includes delivery of the goods to the customer's premises.

Ex works – Prices quoted do not include delivery to the customer's premises. The customer must organise and pay for the delivery of the goods.

Cash on delivery – The customer is expected to pay for the goods when they are delivered.

11.1 Introduction

Credit note – Document issued by a supplier to a customer cancelling part or all of a sales invoice. Business normally issues a credit note:

- when a customer has returned faulty or damaged goods

- when a customer has returned perfect goods by agreement with the supplier

- to make a refund for short deliveries

- to settle a dispute with a customer.

A credit note is the reversal of a previous invoice or part of the invoice value.

Credit notes are issued as documentary evidence that goods have been returned and that all or part of a previous sales invoice is cancelled. Therefore a business must keep strict control over the credit notes it issues.

11.2 Return of goods

When a supplier receives returned goods they must be inspected, counted and recorded on receipt. They would normally be recorded on a returns inwards note.

In the perspective of a customer who is returning goods and consequently receives a credit note exactly the same checks should be made on credit notes as on invoices. The reason for the credit note and the amount that has been credited should be checked, so should all of the calculations and the VAT.

11.3 Authorising credit notes

All credit notes must be authorised by a supervisor prior to being issued to the customer.

Some credit notes may be issued without a returns inwards note. For example, an error may have been made in pricing on an invoice but the customer is satisfied with the goods and does not need to return them.

These credit notes must be issued only after written authorisation has been received and must be reviewed and approved before being sent to the customer or recorded.

11.4 Preparing credit notes

A credit note is effectively the reverse of an invoice and therefore will tend to include all the details that would normally appear on a sales invoice.

If Alpha Ltd (as seen earlier in the chapter) returned two of the chipboard panels, the credit note would be as follows.

City Woods Suppliers

192 Old Kent Road — *Name and address of issuer of credit note*
London
SE1 8QT

Sequential credit note number

Tel: 020 7248 7009 – Fax: 020 7248 7890

VAT registration number of supplier

Returns inwards note reference

Credit note no: CN 02542
Tax point: 30 September 20X3
VAT reg no: 618 2201 63
Return inwards note no: 01531
Invoice no: 1005673
Account no: AL 6215

Date of credit note

Customer's account code

CREDIT NOTE

Credit to: — *Name and address of customer*

Alpha Limited
Mountjoy St
London W12 6RS

Date: 30 September 20X3

Description	Code	Quantity	VAT rate %	Unit price £	Amount exclusive of VAT £
Chipboard 6' × 4'	CB0351	2	20	23.00	46.00
				Goods returned total	46.00
					46.00
VAT				*VAT charged*	9.20
				Total amount of credit	55.20

Rate of VAT on goods returned

12 Coding

12.1 Introduction

Invoices should be coded to show:

- product group/type for analysis of sales/purchases

- customer/supplier account number.

There are several different systems of coding which can be used by a business.

12.2 Sequence codes

Allocate a number, or a letter, to items in a simple list.

For example:

Code	Name
01	ADAMS, Joan
02	AITKEN, James
03	ALCOCK, Freda
04	BROWN, Joe

12.3 Block codes

These allocate bands of numbers to particular categories.

For example, consider a tobacco manufacturer who produces several types of cigarettes, cigars and pipe tobaccos. He could assign a code to each particular brand as follows:

Product type	Block code
Cigarette	01 – 19
Cigar	20 – 29
Pipe tobacco	30 – 39

12.4 Significant digit codes

These are a particular type of group classification code where individual digits and letters are used to represent features of the coded item. The example given is one used to describe different kinds of vehicle tyres.

Code	Item
TT67015B	Tube Tyre 670 × 15 Blackwall
LT67015W	Tubeless Tyre 670 × 15 Whitewall

12.5 Faceted codes

Faceted codes are another type of group classification code by which the digits of the code are divided into facets of several digits and each facet represents some attribute of the item being coded. These codes are similar to significant digit codes but are purely numerical.

Example: Faceted code for types of carpet.

Facet 1	=	type of weave (1 digit)	1	=	Cord
			2	=	Twist
			3	=	Short tufted, etc
Facet 2	=	material (1 digit)	1	=	All wool
			2	=	80% wool, 20% nylon
			3	=	50% wool, 50% nylon, etc
Facet 3	=	pattern (2 digits)	01	=	Self colour (plain)
			02	=	Self colour (embossed)
			03	=	Fig leaf, etc
Facet 4	=	colour (2 digits)	01	=	Off white
			02	=	Bright yellow
			03	=	Scarlet, etc

A typical code would be 220302 representing a twist carpet in 80% wool, 20% nylon, pattern fig leaf and colour bright yellow.

Note that a two-digit facet allows up to 100 different codings (00 to 99).

12.6 Decimal codes (or hierarchical codes)

These are yet another form of a group classification code. The most obvious example of a decimal code is the Universal Decimal Code (UDC) devised by Dewey and widely used for the classification of books in libraries. UDC divides all human knowledge into more and more detailed categories as shown.

Code	Item
3	Social science
37	Education
372	Elementary
372.2	Kindergarten
372.21	Methods
372.215	Songs and games

Whatever the coding system that is used it is important for further accounting purposes that the invoices and credit notes are coded according to type of sales and the particular customer.

You may be expected to code items included on sales invoices or credit notes according to a coding system that is given to you in an assessment.

Activity 2

Is the cheque number used in a cheque book an example of a sequential code or a hierarchical code?

13 Summary

In this chapter we have concentrated on the purpose and flow of a range of business documents. Before preparing an invoice it is necessary to ensure that this is for a valid sale by checking the order and delivery details. It is important that we understand the need to check business documents that are received and sent to ensure they agree to relating documents, the calculations are correct in accordance with discounts and the treatment of VAT.

Answers to chapter activities

Activity 1

(i)	£100.00 × 20/100	=	£20.00
(ii)	£250.00 × 20/100	=	£50.00
(iii)	£480.00 × 20/120	=	£80.00
(iv)	£600.00 × 20/120	=	£100.00

Activity 2

A sequential code (the numbers run in sequential order).

14 Test your knowledge

Workbook Activity 3

ABC Ltd uses codes within the accounting system. An extract from the general ledger coding list is given below:

General ledger account	Code number
Equipment	10
Receivables	20
Electricity	30
Purchases	40
Sales	50

Required:

(a) Why are the general ledger codes numbered in steps of 10, rather than 1,2,3,4?

(b) Give 3 examples of the use of code numbers in an accounting system, other than general ledger accounts codes.

(c) Are the following statements true or false?

	TRUE/ FALSE
General ledger codes help when barcoding an item of inventory	
General ledger codes help when filing a financial document	
General ledger codes help trace relevant accounts quickly and easily	
General ledger codes help find the total amount owing to a supplier	

🗒️ Workbook Activity 4

Nethan Builders codes all purchase invoices and credit notes with a supplier code and a general ledger code:

Supplier	Supplier Account Code
Haddow Bros	HAD29
AJ Broom & Company Ltd	AJB14
Jenson Ltd	JEN32
JM Bond & Co	JMB33

Item	General ledger Code
Softwood	GL110
Hardwood	GL112
Sand	GL130
Steel	GL140
Brick	GL145

Required:

For each of the invoices and credit notes shown below select the appropriate supplier account code and general ledger code to be used to code them.

INVOICE

Haddow Bros

Invoice to:
Nethan Builders
Brecon House
Stamford Road
Manchester
M16 4PL

Deliver to:
As above

The White House, Standing Way, Manchester
M13 6FH
Tel: 0161 560 3140
Fax: 0161 560 5140

Invoice no:	033912
Tax point:	22 April 20X1
VAT reg no:	460 3559 71
Purchase order no::	7166

Code	Description	Quantity	VAT rate %	Unit price £	Amount excl of VAT £
PLY8FE1	Plywood Hardwood 2440 × 1220 mm	12 sheets	20	17.80	213.60
					213.60
VAT at 20%					41.86
Total amount payable					255.46
Deduct discount of 2% if paid within 10 days					

INVOICE

Invoice to:
Nethan Builders
Brecon House
Stamford Road
Manchester
M16 4PL

Jenson Ltd
30 Longfield Park, Kingsway, M45 2TP

Invoice no:	47792
Tax point:	22 April 20X1
VAT reg no:	641 3229 45
Purchase order no::	7162

Deliver to:
As above

Code	Description	Quantity	VAT rate %	Unit price £	Amount excl of VAT £
PL432115	Steel rods 32 × 115 mm	14	20	30.25	423.50
PL432140	Steel rods 32 × 138 mm	8	20	33.15	265.20
					688.70
Trade discount 15%					103.30
					585.40
VAT at 20%					113.56
Total amount payable					698.96

Deduct discount of 3% if paid within 14 days

INVOICE

Invoice to:
Nethan Builders
Brecon House
Stamford Road
Manchester
M16 4PL

A J Broom & Company Limited
59 Parkway, Manchester, M2 6EG
Tel: 0161 560 3392
Fax: 0161 560 5322

Invoice no:	046123
Tax point:	22 April 20X1
VAT reg no:	661 2359 07
Purchase order no:	7164

Deliver to:
As above

Code	Description	Quantity	VAT rate %	Unit price £	Amount excl of VAT £
DGS472	SDG Softwood	9.6 m	20	8.44	81.02
CIBF653	BIC Softwood	7	20	12.30	86.10
					167.12
Trade discount 10%					16.71
					150.41
VAT at 20%					30.08
Total amount payable					180.49

CREDIT NOTE

J M Bond & Co

Credit note to:

Nethan Builders
Brecon House
Stamford Road
Manchester
M16 4PL

North Park Industrial Estate, Manchester, M12 4TU
Tel: 0161 561 3214
Fax: 0161 561 3060

Credit note no: 06192
Tax point: 22 April 20X1
VAT no: 461 4367 91
Invoice no: 331624

Code	Description	Quantity	VAT rate %	Unit price £	Amount excl of VAT £
DGSS4163	Structural softwood untreated	6m	20	6.85	41.10
					41.10
Trade discount 20%					8.22
					32.88
VAT at 20%					6.57
Total amount of credit					39.45

Books of prime entry

2

Introduction

In a typical business there will be a great number of transactions to be recorded on a daily basis. Transactions include credit sales and purchases, cash sales, purchases, expenses and other day to day transactions.

These transactions are initially recorded from their source document into the books of prime entry. Books of prime entry may also be referred to as 'day books'.

KNOWLEDGE
Explain the purpose and content of the books of prime entry (1.2)
Outline how the books of prime entry integrate with the double entry bookkeeping system (2.2)

SKILLS
Enter sales invoices and credit notes into books of prime entry using suitable codes (4.3)
Enter supplier invoices and credit notes into books of prime entry using suitable codes (5.2)

CONTENTS
1   The sales day book
2   The sales returns day book
3   The purchases day book
4   The purchases returns day book
5   The cash book
6   The petty cash book

 **The sales day book**

1.1 Introduction

In a typical business there will be a great number of sales transactions to be recorded. If we were to record each transaction individually, the accounts would get cluttered.

In order to simplify the process (and exercise greater control) we divide the recording of the transactions into three parts.

(a) The first part is the books of prime entry. We shall study here the sales day book.

(b) The second part is the general ledger itself where the double entry takes place.

(c) The third part is the sales ledger which contains the individual receivable accounts. (**Note:** The sales ledger is also sometimes referred to as the subsidiary (sales) ledger.)

Sales invoices and cheques are the source documents which will form the basis of accounting entries in all these three parts.

1.2 Books of prime entry – the sales day book (SDB)

The sales day book is simply a list of the sales invoices that are to be processed for a given period (e.g. a week).

In its simplest form, the sales day book will comprise just the names of the customers and the amount of the invoices issued in the week.

The SDB is not part of the double entry; it is not part of the ledger accounts. It is just a list but we shall use it to perform the double entry. Double entry bookkeeping is studied later in this text.

Week 1			
Customer	*Total* £	*VAT* £	*Net* £
X	1,200	200	1,000
Y	2,400	400	2,000
Z	3,600	600	3,000
Total	7,200	1,200	6,000

1.3 The analysed sales day book

The sales day book is usually analysed with 'analysis columns' showing how the total value of each customer's invoice is made up.

SALES DAY BOOK								
Date	Customer	Reference	Invoice number	Total £	VAT £	Product 1 £	Product 2 £	Product 3 £
			TOTALS					

(a) The date and customer columns are self explanatory.

(b) The reference number is the code number of the customer's account in the sales ledger (where individual accounts are held for credit customers known as 'receivables').

(c) The invoice number is the number of the invoice issued for this sale.

(d) The total column is the total value of the goods sold as shown on the invoice:

- after deducting any trade discount that may have been offered

- including VAT.

💡 Example

An invoice to customer A is made up as follows:

	£
Sale of 50 units at £2 per unit	100.00
Less: 20% trade discount	(20.00)
	80.00
VAT (£80 × 20%)	16.00
Total invoice value	96.00

The £96 would be entered in the 'total' column.

(e) The VAT column – this column is the value of the VAT on the invoice – in this case £16.00.

(f) Product 1, 2, etc columns – these are columns that analyse the net sales value (i.e. the total value after deducting VAT) into groupings that are of interest to the business.

In this introductory section we shall not complicate things by considering more than one type of product so that there will only be one column for sales.

In this case the entry in the sales column would be £80.

(g) The total boxes – at the end of a period (say a week or a month) the sales day book is totalled and the total values of each column are written in the total boxes.

The sales day book would therefore look as follows for the example above:

SALES DAY BOOK								
Date	Customer	Reference	Invoice number	Total £	VAT £	Product 1 £	Product 2 £	Product 3 £
	A			96	16	80		
			TOTALS	96	16	80		

1.4 Casting and cross casting

Casting is the way accountants refer to adding a vertical column of figures and cross-casting is the way accountants refer to adding a horizontal row of figures.

It is worth very briefly doing a simple example of this just to show how a valuable check of the accuracy of your additions is provided by these two operations.

Example

The following table of numbers is similar to the contents of accounting records such as the 'sales day book' or the 'analysed cash book' which you will come across as part of your PBKT studies.

This table might represent the sales of products A to E in three geographical areas. We have deliberately chosen some awkward numbers to demonstrate the process.

You should calculate the totals yourself before looking at the solution.

	A	B	C	D	E	Total
UK	221,863	17,327	14,172	189,221	5,863	
USA	17,155	14,327	8,962	27,625	73,127	
Africa	18,627	33,563	62,815	1,003	57,100	
Total						

Solution

	A	B	C	D	E	Total
UK	221,863	17,327	14,172	189,221	5,863	**448,446**
USA	17,155	14,327	8,962	27,625	73,127	**141,196**
Africa	18,627	33,563	62,815	1,003	57,100	**173,108**
Total	**257,645**	**65,217**	**85,949**	**217,849**	**136,090**	**762,750**

2 The sales returns day book

2.1 The sales returns day book

Sales returns are in practice entered in a 'sales returns day book'. This is similar to the sales day book, and the columns are used in the same way. The only difference is that instead of having a column for the invoice number, there is a column for the 'credit note number'. This is because when the goods are received back the business will issue a credit note.

SALES RETURNS DAY BOOK						
Date	Customer	Reference	Credit note number	Total £	VAT £	Sales returns £

2.2 Sales returns in sales day book

In some businesses the level of sales returns are fairly low and therefore it is not justified to keep a separate sales returns day book. In these cases any credit notes that are issued for sales returns are recorded as negative amounts in the sales day book.

3 The purchases day book

3.1 Introduction

As seen earlier in the chapter, credit sales are recorded in the 'sales day book'. In the case of credit purchases, we have the 'purchases day book'.

The purchases day book is simply a list of the purchases invoices that are to be processed for a given period (e.g. a week).

In its simplest form, the purchases day book will comprise just the names of the suppliers and the amount of the invoices received in the week.

The PDB is not part of the double entry; it is not part of the ledger accounts. It is just a list but we shall use it to perform the double entry. It will look something like this:

Week 1			
Supplier	Total £	VAT £	Net £
A	3,600	600	3,000
B	2,400	400	2,000
C	1,200	200	1,000
Total	7,200	1,200	6,000

3.2   The analysed purchases day book

The purchases day book is usually analysed with 'analysis columns' showing how the total value of each supplier's invoice is made up.

PURCHASES DAY BOOK								
Date	Supplier	Reference	Invoice number	Total £	VAT £	Product 1 £	Product 2 £	Product 3 £
			TOTALS					

(a)   The date and supplier columns are self explanatory.

(b)   The reference number is the number of the supplier's account in the purchases ledger.

(c)   The invoice number is the number of the invoice from the supplier.

(d)   The total column is the value of the goods purchased:

- after deducting any trade discount that may have been offered

- including VAT

- and including (i.e. not deducting) any settlement discount that may be offered to the purchaser (we shall not complicate things at this stage by considering this further).

4   The purchases returns day book

4.1   Introduction

Purchases returns are in practice entered in a 'purchases returns day book'. This is similar to the purchases day book, and the columns are used in the same way. The only difference is that instead of having a column for the invoice number, there is a column for the 'credit note number'. This is because when the goods are sent back the business will receive a credit note from the supplier.

PURCHASES RETURNS DAY BOOK						
Date	Supplier	Reference	Credit note number	Total £	VAT £	Purchases returns £

4.2 Purchases returns in purchases day book

In some businesses the level of purchases returns are fairly low and therefore it is not justified to keep a separate purchases returns day book. In these cases any credit notes that are received for purchases returns are recorded as negative amounts in the purchases day book. If this is the case then you will be told that this is the policy of the business. Care should be taken, however, when adding up the columns in the purchases day book as any credit notes must be deducted rather than added in.

5 The cash book

5.1 The cash book

One of the most important books used within a business is the cash book. There are various forms of cash book, a 'two column' and a 'three column' cash book.

Definition

A cash book is a record of cash receipts and payments that is part of the double entry system.

5.2 Two column cash book

A proforma two column cash book is shown below.

CASH BOOK							
Date	Narrative	Cash £	Bank £	Date	Narrative	Cash £	Bank £

Notes:

(a) The left hand side of the cash book represents the 'debit' side – money received.

(b) The right hand side of the cash book represents the 'credit' side – money paid out.

(c) The date column contains the date of the transaction

(d) The narrative column describes the transactions – typically the name of the customer who is paying. It would also contain the sales ledger code of the receivable.

(e) The cash column on the left hand side (debit side) represents cash received, whereas the cash column on the right hand side (credit side) represents cash paid.

(f) The bank column on the left hand side (debit side) represents money received (by cheque or other bank payment) whereas the bank column on the right hand side (credit side) represents money paid (by cheque or other bank payment).

A business may operate a bank current account as a means to settle business transactions. Receipts may be made automatically, in the form of a cheque or cash may be deposited into the current account. Payments may be made by drawing a cheque against the current account or by an automated payment.

To be able to record these bank specific transactions, a separate column must be introduced to the cash book to account for them. This is what leads to the use of a two column cash book; a column for cash transactions and a column for transactions made through the bank current account. Each column represents a separate account, cash account and bank account, each with its own double entry.

As well as being aware of the use of two columns for bank and cash, you should also be aware that a cash book may have additional columns for the purpose of analysing the receipts and payments in terms of sources and types of income and expenditure.

> ### Q Definition
>
> An analysed cash book is a cash book with additional columns for analysing principal sources and payments for cash.

5.3 Three column cash book

The three-column cashbook incorporates the cash discounts for each relevant entry into a third column. At the end of a certain period of time, when the cashbook is balanced off, the totals from these discount columns would then be transferred to the discount accounts in the general ledger. Discounts received are entered in the discounts column on the right hand side (credit side) of the cashbook, and discounts allowed in the discounts column on the left hand side (debit side) of the cashbook.

A proforma three column cash book is shown below.

CASH BOOK

Date	Narrative	Cash £	Bank £	Discount £	Date	Narrative	Cash £	Bank £	Discount £

The purpose of each of the columns is consistent to that of a two column cash book with the addition of the discount columns in both the receipts (debit) side and the payments (credit) side. It is important to note that cash books can be in different formats with different numbers of analysis columns.

We will now focus on the cash receipts book.

5.4   The analysed cash receipts book

A proforma analysed cash receipts book is shown below.

CASH RECEIPTS BOOK							
Date	Narrative	Reference	Total £	VAT £	SLCA £	Cash sales £	Discount allowed £
		TOTALS					

Notes:

(a)   The date column contains the date of the transaction.

(b)   The narrative column describes the transactions – typically the name of the customer who is paying. It would also contain the sales ledger code of the receivable.

(c)   The reference column contains any other information that may be helpful e.g. 'cash', 'cheque', 'BACS' etc.

(d)   The total column contains the total cash received (including any VAT).

(e)   The VAT column contains the VAT on the transaction but not if the VAT has already been entered in the sales day book. This is a tricky point and is dealt with later.

(f)   The SLCA column contains any cash received that has been received from a receivable. The total received including VAT is entered in this column.

(g)   The cash sales and discount allowed columns will be dealt with later.

5.5 The analysed cash payments book

A proforma analysed cash payments book is shown below

CASH PAYMENTS BOOK									
Date	Narrative	Reference	Total £	VAT £	PLCA £	Cash purchases £	Admin £	Rent and rates £	Discount received £
		TOTALS							

Notes:

(a) The date column contains the date of the transaction.

(b) The narrative column describes the transactions. The reference column may include a reference to the source of the information or the code of a supplier being paid.

(c) The total column contains the total cash paid (including any VAT).

(d) The VAT column contains the VAT on the transaction but not if the VAT has already been entered in the purchases day book.

(e) The PLCA column contains any cash paid that has been paid to a supplier. The total paid including VAT is entered in this column.

(f) The cash purchases column contains cash paid for purchases that are not bought on credit. This would be the VAT exclusive amount (net). The VAT element would be accounted for in the VAT column.

(g) We saw with the analysed cash receipts book that nearly all receipts come from receivables or cash sales. In the case of payments, there is a great variety of suppliers who are paid through the cash book – rent and rates, telephone, electricity, marketing, etc. The business will have a separate column for the categories of expense that it wishes to analyse.

(h) The discount received column is a memorandum column that contains details of any cash/settlement discounts received. These discounts will need to be entered into the ledger accounts as we shall see.

6 The petty cash book

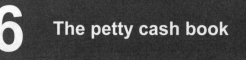

Definition

Petty cash is the small amount of cash that most businesses hold in order to make small cash payments.

6.1 Layout of the petty cash book

The petty cash book is normally set out as a large ledger account with a small receipts side and a larger analysed payments side. A typical petty cash book is set out below.

Receipts			Payments								
Date	Narrative	Total	Date	Narrative	Voucher no	Total	Postage	Cleaning	Tea & Coffee	Sundry	VAT
		£				£	£	£	£	£	£
1 Nov	Bal b/f	35.50									
1 Nov	Cheque 394	114.50	1 Nov	ASDA	58	23.50			23.50		
			2 Nov	Post Office Ltd	59	29.50	29.50				
			2 Nov	Cleaning materials	60	15.07		12.56			2.51
			3 Nov	Postage	61	16.19	16.19				
			3 Nov	ASDA	62	10.57		8.81			1.76
			4 Nov	Newspapers	63	18.90				18.90	
			5 Nov	ASDA	64	12.10				10.09	2.01

6.2 Receipts side of the petty cash book

The receipts side of the petty cash book only requires one column, as the only receipt into the petty cash box is the regular payment into the petty cash box of cash drawn out of the bank account.

From the example of a typical petty cash book (above), we can see that the balance brought forward was £35.50. The petty cash has then been restored up to £150 by paying in an additional £114.50.

6.3   Payments side of the petty cash book

Payments out of the petty cash box will be for a variety of different types of expense and an analysis column is required for each type of expense in the same way as the cash payments book is analysed. The example (above) has split the expenses into postage, cleaning, tea & coffee and sundry expenses.

Note that a column is also required for VAT, as if a petty cash expense includes VAT this must also be analysed out. In addition it is importance to remember that any VAT included in a petty cash expense must be shown separately on the petty cash voucher.

Any VAT shown on the petty cash voucher must be analysed out into the VAT column and the net amount shown in the expense analysis column.

7   Summary

This session has introduced the different books of original entry (day books) that source documents such as invoices and credit notes, are recorded in. It is from these day books that we then go on to post the transactions into the general and subsidiary ledgers. We will now study how to do this by introducing 'double entry bookkeeping'.

KAPLAN PUBLISHING

8 Test your knowledge

Workbook Activity 1

You work in the accounts department of D F Engineering and one of your tasks is to write up the day books. In your organisation there is no separate sales returns day book and therefore any credit notes are entered as negative amounts in the sales day book.

Given below are the details of the sales invoices and credit notes that have been issued this week. D F Engineering does not offer trade or settlement discounts but is registered for VAT and all sales are of standard rated goods.

Invoices sent out:

		Code	£	Invoice number
20X1				
1 May	Fraser & Co	SL14	128.68 plus VAT	03466
	Letterhead Ltd	SL03	257.90 plus VAT	03467
2 May	Jeliteen Traders	SL15	96.58 plus VAT	03468
3 May	Harper Bros	SL22	268.15 plus VAT	03469
	Juniper Ltd	SL17	105.38 plus VAT	03470
4 May	H G Frank	SL30	294.67 plus VAT	03471
5 May	Keller Assocs	SL07	110.58 plus VAT	03472

Credit notes sent out:

		Code	£	Credit note number
20X1				
2 May	Garner & Co	SL12	68.70 plus VAT	0746
4 May	Hill Traders	SL26	117.68 plus VAT	0747

Required:

Write up the sales day book given for the week ending 5 May 20X1 and total all of the columns.

Date	Invoice no	Customer name	Code	Total £	VAT £	Net £

Workbook Activity 2

Stevens Ltd operates an analysed purchases day book, analysing purchases by the geographical area from which the purchases are being made. The areas concerned are:

Zone 1   London region

Zone 2   Scotland region

Zone 3   Other UK

The company is registered for VAT.

Today's date is 14 September 20X2. The company has received the following invoices in the post today:

Supplier	Region	Amount net of VAT £	VAT £
Bradley Ltd	London	210.00	42.00
Hannah Ltd	Wales	470.20	94.04
Spearritt Ltd	London	402.00	80.40
Lee Ltd	Scotland	1,076.00	215.20
O'Meara Ltd	Northern Ireland	317.60	63.52
Cattermole Ltd	Scotland	62.44	12.48
Barrett Ltd	London	107.80	21.56

Required:

Write up the purchases day book given and total all of the columns.

Date	Supplier	Total £	VAT £	Zone 1 £	Zone 2 £	Zone 3 £

Double entry bookkeeping – introduction

3

Introduction

We have reviewed the background to business transactions, looking at the different business documents we may encounter and how we record information from these source documents into the books of prime entry.

This chapter introduces the different business organisations that we may encounter. We then study the basic concepts and rules of bookkeeping. In particular:

- the dual effect principle
- the separate entity principle, and
- the accounting equation.

Together these will show how the assets of a business will always equal its liabilities and pave the way for studying ledger accounting in the next chapter.

KNOWLEDGE	CONTENTS
Explain the accounting equation and how it relates to a double entry bookkeeping system (2.1)	1 Business organisations 2 Types of accounting 3 Basic principles of accounting 4 The accounting equation: examples
Define capital income and capital expenditure (2.5)	
Define revenue income and revenue expenditure (2.6)	

1 Business organisations

1.1 Introduction

A business is an organisation that regularly enters into different transactions. There are three types of business organisations that you should have awareness of for your Level 2 AAT studies:

- Sole traders
- Partnerships
- Companies

1.2 Sole traders

These are organisations that are owned and operated by one person. They tend to be small as they are constrained by the limited financial resources of their owner. Preparing final accounts for sole traders is not assessed until Level 3 'Prepare final accounts for sole traders and partnerships' (FSTP).

1.3 Partnerships

These are organisations owned by two or more persons working in common with a view to making a profit. The greater number of owners compared with a sole trader increases the availability of finance and this is often the reason for forming this structure. Preparing final accounts for partnerships is not assessed until Level 3 'Prepare final accounts for sole traders and partnerships' (FSTP).

1.4 Companies

These are organisations recognised in law as 'persons' in their own right. A company may own assets and incur liabilities in its own name. The accounting of these organisations must meet certain minimum obligations imposed by legislation, for example, via company law and other regulations. Preparing final accounts for companies is not assessed until Level 4 'Financial statements' (FSTM).

2 Types of accounting

2.1 Management accounting and financial accounting

Depending on what purposes the statements are being produced for, the accounts can be referred to as being either **management accounts** or **financial accounts.**

Management accounts

These are usually prepared on a monthly basis to present the financial information in a way that enables the managers to run the business more effectively.

Financial accounts

These are prepared annually, mainly for the benefit of people outside the management of the business, such as the owners of the business (for example, shareholders who have appointed directors to run the business on their behalf), HM Revenue and Customs, banks, customers, suppliers and the government.

In this text we focus on financial accounting principles, though the majority of concepts also apply to management accounting.

2.2 The two main financial statements

The objective of financial accounting is to provide financial information about a business. This information is given in a set of financial statements (or accounts), which consists of two principal statements:

- The **statement of profit or loss.** This is a summary of the business's transactions (income and expense) for a given period.

- The **statement of financial position.** This is a statement of the assets and liabilities of the business at a given date. This date is the end of the period covered by the statement of profit or loss.

These financial statements are the final product of the accounting system of a business and it is useful to be aware of where all of the double entry bookkeeping that you will study in this chapter is leading. However, you do not need to know anything about the format or rules governing the preparation of the financial statements for Level 2.

2.3 Statement of profit or loss – definitions

The following definitions will be used throughout your studies.

Q Definitions

- **Sales revenue** is income generated from the trading activities of the business.

- **Cost of sales** is the cost of buying or producing the goods for resale.

- **Gross profit** is the profit remaining, after the cost of sales have been deducted from sales revenue.

- **Sundry income** – other types of income that aren't generated by the primary trading activities of the business.

- **Expenses** are the day to day running costs of the business.

- **Net profit or loss** – the profit or loss remaining after expenses have been deducted.

2.4 Statement of financial position – definitions

The following definitions will be used throughout your studies.

🔍 Definitions

- An **asset** is something owned by a business, available for use in the business.

- **Non-current asset** – an asset which is to be used for the long term in the business and not resold as part of the trading activities, for example the purchase of a delivery van.

- **Current asset** – a short-term asset of the business which is to be used in the business in the near future i.e. cash or something that will soon be converted into cash.

- A **receivable** is an example of a current asset. A receivable is someone who owes the business money i.e. a credit customer.

- **Non-current liability** – an amount owed by the business and due to be paid in the longer term (after 12 months).

- A **liability** is an amount owed by the business, i.e. an obligation to pay money at some future date.

- A **payable** is an example of a liability. A payable is someone the business owes money to i.e. a credit supplier.

- **Capital** is the amount which the owner has invested in the business; this is owed back to the owner and is therefore a special liability of the business.

- **Drawings** are amounts withdrawn by the owner for their own personal use: drawings may be of cash or items of inventory.

A typical statement of profit or loss is shown below.

Statement of profit or loss for the year-ended 31 December 20X2

	£	£
Sales revenue		X
Less: Cost of sales		
Inventory on 1 January (opening inventory)	X	
Add: Purchases of goods	X	
	X	
Less: Inventory on 31 December (closing inventory)	(X)	
		(X)
Gross profit		X
Sundry income:		
Discounts received	X	
Commission received	X	
Rent received	X	
		X
		X
Less: Expenses:		
Rent	X	
Rates	X	
Lighting and heating	X	
Telephone	X	
Postage	X	
Insurance	X	
Stationery	X	
Payroll expenses	X	
Accountancy fees	X	
Bank charges and interest	X	
Irrecoverable debts	X	
Delivery costs	X	
Van running expenses	X	
Selling expenses	X	
Discounts allowed	X	
		(X)
Profit/(loss) for the year		X/(X)

An example of a typical sole trader's statement of financial position is given below:

Statement of financial position as at 31 December 20X2

	Cost £	Depreciation £	CV £
Non-current assets			
Freehold factory	X	X	X
Machinery	X	X	X
Motor vehicles	X	X	X
	X	X	X
Current assets			
Inventories		X	
Trade receivables		X	
Cash at bank		X	
Cash in hand		X	
		X	
Current liabilities			
Trade payables		(X)	
Net current assets			X
Total assets less current liabilities			X
Non-current liabilities			
Loan			(X)
Net assets			X
Capital at 1 January			X
Net profit for the year			X
			X
Less: Drawings			(X)
Proprietor's funds			X

2.5　The difference between 'cash' and 'bank'

A possible confusion in terminology is caused by the apparent interchangeable use of the words 'cash' and 'bank'.

The normal use of the words suggests that a bank account operates by paying money out of the account with a cheque and paying either cash or cheques into the account. In practice you cannot pay 'cash' out of a bank account.

However, accounting terminology does not stick to this distinction, and the terms cash and bank are for the most part, interchangeable. Thus the bank account is often referred to as the 'cash book'. Similarly we will often refer to someone 'taking cash out of the bank' or we will say things like 'John bought a car for £5,000 cash', whereas in reality John would have paid for the car using a cheque.

For the early part of your studies all movements of cash/cheques shall be made through the bank account and references to 'cash' or 'cheques' effectively mean the same thing.

2.6　Capital and revenue

You must also be able to define capital expenditure, revenue expenditure, capital income and revenue income.

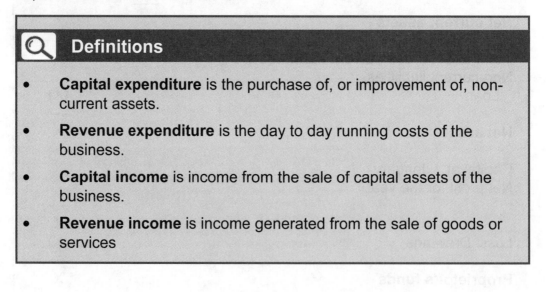

> ### Definitions
>
> - **Capital expenditure** is the purchase of, or improvement of, non-current assets.
>
> - **Revenue expenditure** is the day to day running costs of the business.
>
> - **Capital income** is income from the sale of capital assets of the business.
>
> - **Revenue income** is income generated from the sale of goods or services

 **Basic principles of accounting**

3.1 Introduction

Double entry bookkeeping is based upon three basic principles:

- the dual effect principle
- the separate entity principle
- the accounting equation.

3.2 The dual effect principle

This states that every transaction has two financial effects.

(a) If, for example, you spend £2,000 on a car and pay for it by a cheque, you will have £2,000 less money in the bank, but you will also have acquired an asset worth £2,000.

(b) Again, if you owe a payable £100 and send him a cheque for that amount, you will owe £100 less than before, but you will have £100 less money in the bank.

3.3 The separate entity principle

This states that the owner of a business is, for accounting purposes, a completely separate entity from the business itself. Therefore the money that the owner pays into the business as initial capital has to be accounted for as an amount that the business owes back to the owner. In just the same way, any money that the owner takes out of the business, known as 'drawings', is treated as a reduction of the initial capital that is owed back to the owner.

The dual effect principle works here as well. If the owner of the business pays £5,000 into his business, one effect is that the business has £5,000 more cash and the second effect is that the business has a £5,000 liability (called 'capital').

Note that we look at this from the **point of view of the business**, not from the owner's point of view. This is because when studying bookkeeping we are only interested in the business – we are not considering the owner's personal finances.

3.4 The accounting equation

At its simplest, the accounting equation simply says that:

Assets = Liabilities

If we treat the owner's capital as a special form of liability then the accounting equation is:

Assets = Liabilities + Capital

Or, rearranging:

Assets – Liabilities = Capital

Profit will increase the proprietor's capital and drawings will reduce it, so that we can write the equation as:

Assets – Liabilities = Capital + Profit – Drawings

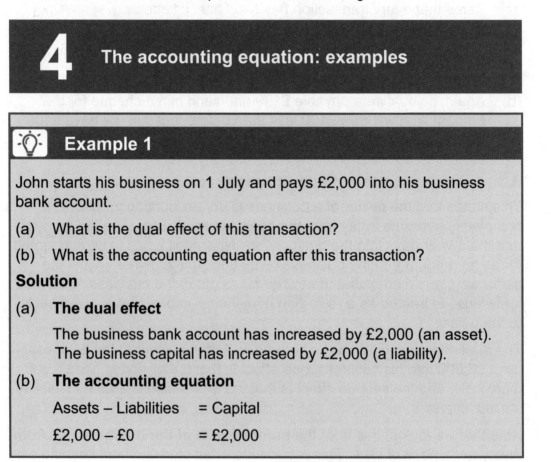

4 The accounting equation: examples

Example 1

John starts his business on 1 July and pays £2,000 into his business bank account.

(a) What is the dual effect of this transaction?

(b) What is the accounting equation after this transaction?

Solution

(a) **The dual effect**

The business bank account has increased by £2,000 (an asset). The business capital has increased by £2,000 (a liability).

(b) **The accounting equation**

Assets – Liabilities   = Capital

£2,000 – £0   = £2,000

Example 2

Percy started business on 1 January by paying £20,000 into a business bank account. He then spent £500 on a second-hand van by cheque, £1,000 on purchases of inventory for cash, took £500 cash for his own use and bought goods on credit costing £400.

What are the two effects of each of these transactions?

What would the accounting equation look like after each of these transactions?

Solution

(a) **Percy pays £20,000 into a business bank account**

The bank balance increases from zero to £20,000 (an asset) and the business now has capital of £20,000 (a liability). Capital is the amount that is owed back to the owner of the business, Percy.

Accounting equation:

Assets – Liabilities = Capital

£20,000 – £0   = £20,000

(b) **Percy buys a second-hand van for £500 by cheque**

The bank balance decreases by £500 (a reduction of assets) but the business has acquired a new £500 asset, the van.

The van is a specific type of asset known as a non-current asset as it is for long-term use in the business rather than an asset that is likely to be sold in the trading activities of the business.

The assets of the business are now:

	£
Van	500
Bank (20,000 – 500)	19,500
	————
	20,000
	————

The liabilities and capital are unchanged.

Accounting equation:

Assets – Liabilities = Capital

£20,000 – £0   = £20,000

(c) **Percy spends £1,000 on purchases of goods for cash**

The bank balance goes down by £1,000 but the business has another asset, inventory of £1,000.

Inventory is a short-term asset as it is due to be sold to customers in the near future and is known as a current asset.

The assets of the business are now:

	£
Van	500
Inventory	1,000
Bank (19,500 – 1,000)	18,500
	20,000

Accounting equation:

Assets – Liabilities = Capital

£20,000 – £0   = £20,000

(d) **Percy took £500 of cash out of the business**

The bank balance has decreased by £500 and capital has also decreased as the owner has taken money out of the business – this is known as drawings.

Remember that the owner is a completely separate entity from the business itself and if he takes money out of the business in the form of drawings then this means that the business owes him less.

The assets of the business are now:

	£
Van	500
Inventory	1,000
Bank (18,500 – 500)	18,000
	19,500

The capital of the business is now £(20,000 – 500) = £19,500.

Accounting equation:

Assets – Liabilities = Capital

£19,500 – £0   = £19,500

(e) Purchased goods on credit for £400

The asset of inventory increases by £400 and the business now has a liability of £400, the amount that is owed to the credit supplier. A liability is an amount that is owed by the business.

The assets of the business are now:

	£
Van	500
Inventory (1,000 + 400)	1,400
Bank	18,000
	─────
	19,900
	─────

The liability of the business is £400. The capital is unchanged.

Accounting equation:

Assets – Liabilities = Capital

£19,900 – £400   = £19,500

General notes:

1   Each and every transaction that a business undertakes has two effects. The accounting equation reflects the two effects of each transaction and the accounting equation should always balance.

2   The owner is a completely separate entity from the business, any money the owner puts into the business is known as capital and any amounts taken out by the owner are known as drawings.

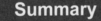

5 Summary

You must understand the basic definitions covered in this chapter. You must also understand the principles of dual effect and separate entity. The accounting equation underlies the whole of bookkeeping and it is imperative that you fully understand these foundations which will be built on further. Re-work the examples in this chapter if necessary.

6 Test your knowledge

Workbook Activity 1

(a) State whether each of the following are an asset or a liability:

(i) Money in the business bank account

(ii) A payable

(iii) Inventory of goods for resale

(iv) A computer used in the accounts department

(v) A receivable

(vi) A salesman's car

(b) Name 3 different parties who would be interested in financial statements.

(c) Name the 3 basic principles of double entry bookkeeping and briefly describe each.

Workbook Activity 2

Required:

Show the two effects of each of these transactions and what the accounting equation would look like after each of these transactions.

1   **Introduce capital**

Example 1

You win £10,000 and use it to create a retail business (called TLC) selling hearts and roses. What is the effect?

Answer 1

Dual effect

The business has cash of	£10,000	(asset)
The business owes you	£10,000	(capital)

TLC's position is:

Assets	Capital
£	£

(In this first example, we recorded the dual effect for you just to get you started. In later examples you will need to enter the dual effect yourself, as well as TLC's position after the transaction.)

2 Buy inventory with cash

Example 2

TLC buys 500 chocolate hearts. The cost of each heart is £5. What is the effect?

Answer 2

Dual effect

TLC's position is:

Assets	Capital
£	£

3 Buy inventory on credit

In reality a business will not always pay for its purchases with cash but is more likely to buy items on credit. When goods are bought on credit, a liability of the business called a **payable** is generated.

Example 3

TLC buys inventory of 200 red roses on credit. Each red rose costs £10. What is the effect?

Answer 3

Dual effect

TLC's position is:

Net assets	Capital
£	£

4   **Buy a delivery van**

The delivery van is bought for ongoing use within the business rather than for resale. Such assets are known as **non-current assets.**

Example 4

TLC buys a delivery van for £1,000 cash. What is the effect?

Answer 4

Dual effect

TLC's position is:

Net assets £	Capital £

5   **Sell inventory for profit**

Example 5

TLC sells 200 red roses for £15 cash each. What is the effect?

Answer 5

Dual effect

TLC's position is:

Net assets £	Capital £

6   **Sell inventory (on credit) for profit**

It is equally likely that a business will sell goods on credit. When goods are sold on credit, an asset of the business called a **receivable** is generated.

Example 6

TLC sells 400 chocolate hearts to Valentino for £12.50 each on credit. What is the effect?

Answer 6

Dual effect

TLC's position is:

Net assets	Capital
£	£

7 Pay expenses

Example 7

In reality, TLC will have been incurring expenses from its commencement. TLC received and paid a gas bill for £500. What is the effect?

Answer 7

Dual effect

TLC's position is:

Net assets	Capital
£	£

8 Take out a loan

In order to fund your future expansion plans for TLC, you persuade your Aunt to lend TLC £2,000.

Example 8

TLC is lent £2,000 cash by your Aunt. She expects to be repaid in two years' time. What is the effect?

Answer 8

Dual effect

TLC's position is:

Net assets	Capital
£	£

9 Payment to payables for purchases

Example 9

TLC pays cash of £1,500 towards the £2,000 owed to the supplier. What is the effect?

Answer 9

Dual effect

TLC's position is:

Net assets	Capital
£	£

10 Receive cash from receivables

Example 10

TLC's receivable sends a cheque for £3,000. What is the effect?

Answer 10

Dual effect

TLC's position is:

Net assets	Capital
£	£

11 Drawings

Example 11

You withdraw £750 from the business. Such a withdrawal is merely a repayment of the capital you introduced. Your withdrawal is called **drawings.** What is the effect?

Answer 11

Dual effect

TLC's position is:

Net assets	Capital
£	£

Workbook Activity 3

Bertie Wooster started a business as an antique dealer on 1 July 20X9.

Required:

Show the accounting equation which results from each of the following transactions made during Bertie's first two weeks of trading.

(a)   Started the business with £5,000 in cash as opening capital.

(b)   Bought an Edwardian desk for £500 cash.

(c)   Bought five art deco table lamps for £200 each, on credit from Roderick Spode.

(d)   Sold the desk for £750 cash.

(e)   Sold four of the table lamps for £300 each on credit to his Uncle Tom.

(f)   Paid rent of £250 cash.

(g)   Drew £100 in cash out of the business for living expenses.

(h)   Earned £50 for writing a magazine article, but had not yet been paid for it.

(i)   Paid Roderick Spode £500 on account.

(j)   Received £1,200 from Uncle Tom in full settlement of the amount due.

(k)   Bought a van for use in the business for £4,000 cash.

(l)   Received a telephone bill for £150 but did not pay it yet.

Note: Each transaction follows on from the one before.

Ledger accounting

4

Introduction

In the first two chapters of this text we looked at different business documents and how these documents are entered into the books of prime entry. In the third chapter we reviewed the basic concepts and principles underlying double entry bookkeeping.

Before we review how details from the books of prime entry are entered into the accounting system we shall introduce how to record basic transactions in a 'ledger account' as part of the 'general ledger'. We will also learn how to balance of a ledger account and how those balances are brought together for the trial balance.

SKILLS
Total and balance ledger accounts, clearly showing balances carried down and brought down (8.2)
Extract an initial trial balance (8.3)

CONTENTS

1 Ledger accounting
2 Worked example
3 Additional example
4 Credit purchases
5 Credit sales
6 Procedure for balancing a ledger account
7 The trial balance

1 Ledger accounting

1.1 Introduction

The accounting equation introduced in Chapter 3 has limitations. Although we are able to calculate a profit figure, we are unable to determine which part of the profit are sales and which part are expenses. To be able to make this determination, we will now account for the movement in sales and purchases, rather than simply the movement of inventory.

Another limitation of the accounting equation is that in practice it would be far too time consuming to write up the accounting equation each time that the business undertakes a transaction. Instead the two effects of each transaction are recorded in ledger accounts.

1.2 The ledger account

A typical ledger account is shown below:

Title of account							
DEBIT				CREDIT			
Date	Details	Folio	Amount £	Date	Details	Folio	Amount £

The important point to note is that it has two sides. The left hand side is known as the **debit** side **(Dr)** and the right hand side is known as the **credit** side **(Cr).**

- The date column contains the date of the transaction.

- The details column (can also be referred to as the narrative column) usually contains the title of the other account that holds the second part of the dual effect. It may also have a brief description of the nature of the entry (e.g. 'rent 1.1.X3 to 31.3.X3').

- The folio column contains a reference to the source of the information, for example, 'sales day book p17' or 'payroll month 6'. You may not always see the folio column being used within a ledger account.

- The amount column simply contains the monetary value of the transaction.

- The title of the account is a name that reflects the nature of the transaction ('van account', 'bank account', 'electricity account', etc).

The importance of completing the ledger account correctly, in terms of the presentation, should not be underestimated. Vital marks can be gained in the exam by ensuring all details, including the date and narrative are completed accurately.

1.3 Simplified account

The ledger account in 1.2 is very detailed and in much of this book we use a simpler form of the account. Part of the reason for this is that it is easier to 'see' the entries being made if there is less detail in the accounts. Thus, we sometimes do without the date or folio to keep things clear and simple.

For example, we will often use accounts which look like this:

Bank account			
	£	Van	£
			500

Van account			
	£		£
Bank	500		

1.4 The golden rule for making entries in the ledger accounts

The golden rule for making entries in ledger accounts is:

Every debit entry must have an equal and opposite credit entry.

This reflects the dual effect of each transaction and ensures the accounting equation always balances.

It is also why we refer to the process as 'double entry bookkeeping'.

1.5   Which accounts to debit and credit?

The mnemonic 'DEAD/CLIC' is a good way to help determine if an entry should be made on the debit side or on the credit side of a ledger account.

Ledger account	
Debits increase:	**Credits increase:**
Expenses	**L**iabilities
Assets	**I**ncome
Drawings	**C**apital

We need to appreciate the effect a debit or a credit entry will have.

Ledger account	
A **debit entry** represents:	A **credit entry** represents:
• An increase in the value of an asset	• A decrease in the value of an asset
• A decrease in the value of a liability	• An increase in the value of a liability
• An increase to an item of expenditure	• An increase to an item of income (revenue)
• A decrease to an item of income	• A decrease to an item of expense.

1.6   What goes on the debit or credit side?

Example (part 1)

If John pays £2,000 into his business bank account as capital, we need to ask a number of questions to determine the double entry required.

(a)   **Which** accounts are affected?

(b)   What **type** of accounts are they i.e. asset/liability/income/expense?

(c)   Is the transaction **increasing or decreasing** the account?

So let's consider these questions for John's investment of capital into his business.

(a)   The accounts that are affected are the bank account and the capital account.

(b)   The bank account is an asset whereas the capital is a special kind of liability.

(c)   As we have paid money into the bank account, the asset is increasing – therefore a debit entry is required.

As John (the owner) has invested £2,000 into the business, the business owes him this amount back. This is an increase to a liability – therefore a credit entry is required.

To summarise:

Debit   Bank account

Credit   Capital account

Bank account			
	£		£
Capital	2,000		

Capital account			
	£		£
		Bank	2,000

Example (part 2)

If John's business now pays £1,000 out of the bank to buy a van, considering the questions again:

(a)   The accounts that are affected are the bank account and the van account.

(b)   The bank account is an asset and the van account is also an asset (a non-current asset).

(c)   As we have paid money out of the bank account, the asset is decreasing – therefore a credit entry is required.

The business has acquired a van, which is a non-current asset, this is an increase to an asset – therefore a debit entry is required.

To summarise:

Debit   Van account

Credit   Bank account

Bank account			
	£		£
Capital	2,000	Van	1,000

Capital account			
	£		£
		Bank	2,000

Van account			
	£		£
Bank	1,000		

2   Worked example

2.1   Introducing capital into the business – explanation

The owner of a business starts the business by paying money into the business bank account. This is the capital of the business. The business will need this money to 'get going'. It may need to pay rent, buy inventory for sale or pay wages to its staff before it has actually generated money itself through making sales.

Example

Frankie starts a business and pays £5,000 into the business bank account. What is the double entry for this transaction?

Solution

- £5,000 has been paid into the bank account.

  It represents an asset of the business.

  This is therefore a debit in the bank account.

- The business has a liability because it owes Frankie (the owner) £5,000.

  This liability will be a credit in the capital account.

Bank			Capital		
Capital	£5,000			Bank	£5,000

2.2 Purchasing goods for resale

A business buys goods for resale to customers – that is how most businesses (e.g. shops) make their money. These goods (known as 'inventory') are assets which the business owns (until the inventory is sold). Buying inventory is referred to as making a 'purchase' which is a type of expense.

Example

Frankie buys £300 of chocolate bars for resale. He pays with a cheque to his supplier.

What is the double entry for this transaction?

Solution

- The business has paid £300 out of its bank account.

  Therefore, the £300 will be credited to the bank account.

- Buying the chocolate bars (inventory) is known as making a purchase (a type of expense).

  This expense will be debited to the purchases account.

Purchases			Bank		
Bank	£300			Purchases	£300

2.3 Paying office rent

A business will typically rent premises in order to carry out its operations. It will pay rent to the landlord of the premises. Rent is an expense of the business.

Example

Frankie pays £1,000 per quarter for the rent of his offices. He pays with a cheque to the landlord.

What is the double entry for this transaction?

Solution

- The business has paid £1,000 out of its bank account.

  Therefore, the £1,000 will be credited to the bank account.

- The rent is an expense.

  This expense will be debited to the rent account.

Rent				Bank	
Bank	£1,000			Rent	£1,000

2.4 Buying stationery

A business will buy stationery in order to be able to operate. The items of stationery (pens, paper, etc) are not for resale to customers but they tend to be used quickly after they are purchased. Therefore, stationery tends to be classified as an expense of the business, as opposed to an asset.

Example

Frankie pays £200 for items of stationery. He pays with a cheque to the supplier.

What is the double entry for this transaction?

Solution

- The business has paid £200 out of its bank account.

  Therefore, the £200 will be credited to the bank account.

- The stationery is an expense.

  This expense will be debited to the stationery account.

Stationery		Bank	
Bank £200			Stationery £200

2.5 Buying a computer

A business will buy computers in order to streamline its operations. These computers are not bought with a view to re-sale and are to be used in the business for the long term. They are therefore a non-current asset of the business.

Example

Frankie pays £900 to purchase a computer. He pays with a cheque to the supplier.

What is the double entry for this transaction?

Solution

- Once again start with the bank account.

  The business has paid £900 out of its bank account.

  Therefore, the £900 will be credited to the bank account.

- The computer is a non-current asset.

  The £900 will be debited to the non-current asset computer account.

Computer		Bank	
Bank £900			Computer £900

2.6 Receiving income from sales of goods

A business will sell the goods it has purchased for re-sale. This is income for the business and is referred to as 'sales'. You may also hear the terms 'revenue' or 'sales revenue'.

Example

Frankie sells goods for £1,500. The customer pays cash.

What is the double entry for this transaction?

Solution

- Once again start with the bank account.

  The business has received £1,500 into its bank account.

  Therefore, the £1,500 will be debited to the bank account.

- The cash received is income.

  This income will be credited to the sales account.

Sales			Bank		
	Bank	£1,500	Sales	£1,500	

2.7 Receiving income for services provided

A business may provide services to its customers, e.g.it may provide consultancy advice. This is income for the business and will usually be referred to as 'sales'.

Example

Frankie provides consultancy services to a client who pays £2,000 in cash. What is the double entry for this transaction?

Solution

- Once again start with the bank account.

  The business has received £2,000 into its bank account.

  Therefore, the £2,000 will be debited to the bank account.

- The cash received is income.

  This income will be credited to the sales account.

Sales			Bank		
	Bank	£2,000	Sales	£2,000	

KAPLAN PUBLISHING

3 Additional example

Example

Percy started business on 1 January and made the following transactions.

1   Paid £20,000 into a business bank account.

2   Spent £500 on a second-hand van.

3   Paid £1,000 on purchases of inventory.

4   Took £50 cash for his own personal use.

5   On 5 January bought goods for cash costing £500.

6   Made sales for cash of £2,000.

7   On 15 January paid £200 of rent.

Task 1

Show how the debit and credit entries for each transaction are determined.

Task 2

Enter the transactions into the relevant ledger accounts.

Solution

Task 1

(1)   *Capital invested*

Percy has paid £20,000 into the bank account – therefore the bank account is debited.

Debit (Dr)   Bank   £20,000

The business now owes the owner £20,000. Capital is the amount owed by the business to its owner – this is a liability, therefore a credit entry is required in the capital account.

Credit (Cr)   Capital   £20,000

(2) *Purchase of van*

The business has paid £500 out of the bank account – therefore a credit entry in the bank account.

Cr Bank £500

The business now has a van costing £500 – this is an asset therefore a debit entry in the van account. This is a non-current asset of the business.

Dr Van £500

(3) *Purchase of inventory for cash*

The business has paid out £1,000 out of the bank account – therefore a credit to the bank account.

Cr Bank £1,000

The business has made purchases of inventory costing £1,000 – this is an item of expenditure therefore a debit entry in the purchases account. Note that the debit entry is to a purchases account not a inventory account. The inventory account is a different account altogether and inventory movements will be considered later.

Dr Purchases £1,000

(4) *Drawings*

The business has paid £50 out of the bank account – therefore credit the bank account.

Cr Bank £50

The proprietor has made drawings of £50 – this is a reduction of capital and therefore a debit entry to the drawings account.

Dr Drawings £50

Drawings should not be directly debited to the capital account. A separate drawings account should be used.

(5) *Purchase of goods for cash*

The business has paid out £500 – therefore credit the bank account.

Cr Bank £500

The business has made purchases of inventory costing £500 – an expense therefore debit the purchases account.

Dr Purchases £500

(6) *Sale for cash*

The business has paid £2,000 into the bank account – therefore a debit to the bank account.

Dr	Bank	£2,000

The business has made sales of £2,000 – this is income therefore a credit to the sales account.

Cr	Sales	£2,000

(7) *Payment of rent*

The business now paid £200 out of the bank account – therefore a credit to the bank account.

Cr	Bank	£200

The business has incurred an expense of rent – as an expense item the rent account must be debited.

Dr	Rent	£200

Task 2

Bank

Date			£	Date			£
1 Jan	Capital	(1)	20,000	1 Jan	Van	(2)	500
5 Jan	Sales	(6)	2,000		Purchases	(3)	1,000
					Drawings	(4)	50
				5 Jan	Purchases	(5)	500
				15 Jan	Rent	(7)	200

Capital

Date			£	Date			£
				1 Jan	Bank	(1)	20,000

Van

Date			£	Date			£
1 Jan	Bank	(2)	500				

Purchases

Date			£	Date		£
1 Jan	Bank	(3)	1,000			
5 Jan	Bank	(5)	500			

Drawings

Date			£	Date		£
1 Jan	Bank	(4)	50			

Sales

Date		£	Date			£
			5 Jan	Bank	(6)	2,000

Rent

Date			£	Date		£
15 Jan	Bank	(7)	200			

Activity 1

Write up the following cash transactions in the ledger accounts.

Transaction	Details
1	Set up the business by introducing £150,000 in cash.
2	Purchase property costing £140,000. Pay in cash.
3	Purchase goods costing £5,000. Pay in cash.
4	Sell goods for £7,000. All cash sales.
5	Purchase goods costing £8,000. Pay in cash.
6	Pay a sundry expense of £100, by cheque.
7	Sell goods for £15,000. All cash sales.
8	Pay wages of £2,000 to an employee.
9	Pay postage costs of £100, by cheque.

4 Credit purchases

Definitions

A cash purchase occurs when goods are bought (or a service received) and the customer pays immediately using cash, cheques or credit cards. A receipt is issued for the amount of cash paid.

A credit purchase occurs when goods are bought (or a service received) and the customer does not have to pay immediately but can pay after a specified number of days. An invoice is then issued to request that payment is made.

Example

We have already seen the double entry for a cash purchase and we shall now contrast this with the double entry for a credit purchase by means of an illustration.

John buys goods from Sam for £2,000.

(a) Record the double entry in John's books if John pays for the goods immediately with a cheque.

(b) Record the double entry in John's books if John buys the goods on credit and pays some time later.

Solution

(a) **Cash purchase**

The double entry is simply to:

Credit the bank account with £2,000 because £2,000 has been paid out.

Debit the purchases account with £2,000 because goods have been purchased with £2,000.

Bank

	£		£
		Purchases	2,000

Purchases

	£		£
Bank	2,000		

(b) **Credit purchase**

We have to record two transactions separately:

(i) *At the time the purchase is made*

At the time the purchase is made we debit £2,000 to the purchases account because a purchase has been made, but we do not make any entry in the bank account yet, because at that point, no cash has been paid. The other effect is that John has a liability, he owes £2,000 to the supplier, Sam, who we can refer to as a payable.

The double entry is:

Debit the purchases account with £2,000 because expenses have increased by £2,000.

Credit payables account with £2,000 (this is a liability of the business).

Purchases

	£		£
Payables	2,000		

Payables

	£		£
		Purchases	2,000

(ii) *When John pays the £2,000*

The double entry now will be:

Credit the bank account with £2,000 because £2,000 has been paid out.

Debit the payable account because John has paid and the payable has been reduced by £2,000.

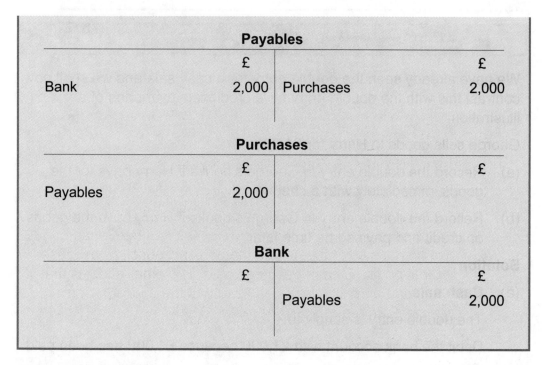

Payables

	£		£
Bank	2,000	Purchases	2,000

Purchases

	£		£
Payables	2,000		

Bank

	£		£
		Payables	2,000

4.1 Summary

The net effect of the above credit purchase is that the payable has a nil balance because John has paid, and we are left with a debit in the purchases account and a credit in the cash book. This is exactly as for a cash purchase – we just had to go through the intermediate step of the payables account to get there.

5 Credit sales

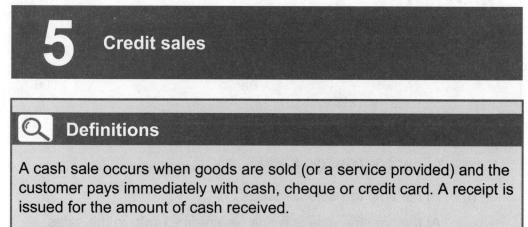

Definitions

A cash sale occurs when goods are sold (or a service provided) and the customer pays immediately with cash, cheque or credit card. A receipt is issued for the amount of cash received.

A credit sale occurs when goods are sold (or a service provided) and the customer does not have to pay immediately but can pay after a specified number of days. An invoice is issued to request that the balance owed is then paid.

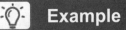 **Example**

We have already seen the double entry for a cash sale and we shall now contrast this with the double entry for a credit sale by means of an illustration.

George sells goods to Harry for £1,000.

(a)   Record the double entry in George's books if Harry pays for the goods immediately with a cheque.

(b)   Record the double entry in George's books if Harry buys the goods on credit and pays some time later.

Solution

(a)   **Cash sale**

The double entry is simply to:

Debit the bank account with £1,000 because £1,000 has been paid in.

Credit the sales account with £1,000 because income has increased by £1,000.

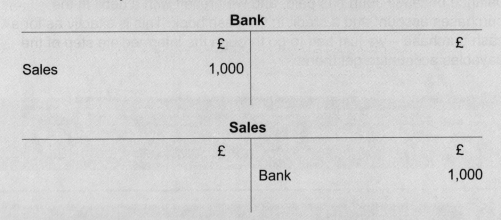

		Bank			
		£			£
Sales		1,000			

		Sales			
		£			£
			Bank		1,000

(b)   **Credit sale**

The double entry will be made at two separate times.

(i)   *At the time the sale is made*

At the time the sale is made we credit £1,000 to the sales account because a sale has been made, but we cannot make any entry in the bank account at the time of the sale because no cash is received. However, the dual effect principle means that there must be another effect to this transaction, and in this case it is that the business has acquired a receivable.

The double entry is:

Debit receivables account with £1,000 (this is an asset of the business).

Credit the sales account with £1,000 because income has increased by £1,000.

Receivables

	£		£
Sales	1,000		

Sales

	£		£
		Receivables	1,000

(ii)   *When Harry pays the £1,000*

The double entry now will be:

Debit the bank account with £1,000 because £1,000 has been paid in.

Credit the receivables account because Harry has paid and the receivable has been reduced by £1,000.

Receivables

	£		£
Sales	1,000	Bank	1,000

Sales

	£		£
		Receivables	1,000

Bank

	£		£
Receivables	1,000		

5.1 Summary

The net effect of the above credit sale is that the receivable has a nil balance because Harry has paid and we are left with a credit in the sales account and a debit in the cash book. This is exactly as for a cash sale – we just had to go through the intermediate step of the receivable account to get there.

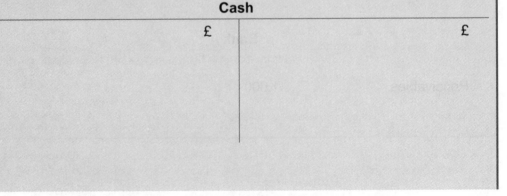

Activity 2

We shall now revisit the activity TLC from Chapter 3 and record the transactions with debits and credits to ledger accounts.

Date	Detail
1.1.X5	TLC commenced business with £10,000 cash introduced by you, the proprietor
2.1.X5	TLC bought inventory of 500 chocolate hearts for £2,500 cash
3.1.X5	TLC bought inventory of 200 red roses on credit for £2,000
4.1.X5	TLC bought a delivery van for £1,000 cash
5.1.X5	TLC sold all the red roses for £3,000 cash
6.1.X5	TLC sold 400 chocolate hearts for £5,000 on credit
7.1.X5	TLC paid a gas bill for £500 cash
8.1.X5	TLC took out a loan of £2,000
9.1.X5	TLC paid £1,500 cash to trade payables
10.1.X5	TLC received £3,000 cash from receivables
11.1.X5	The proprietor withdrew £750 cash

Required:

Record these transactions in the relevant ledger accounts. Make your entries in the ledger accounts below.

Cash

	£		£

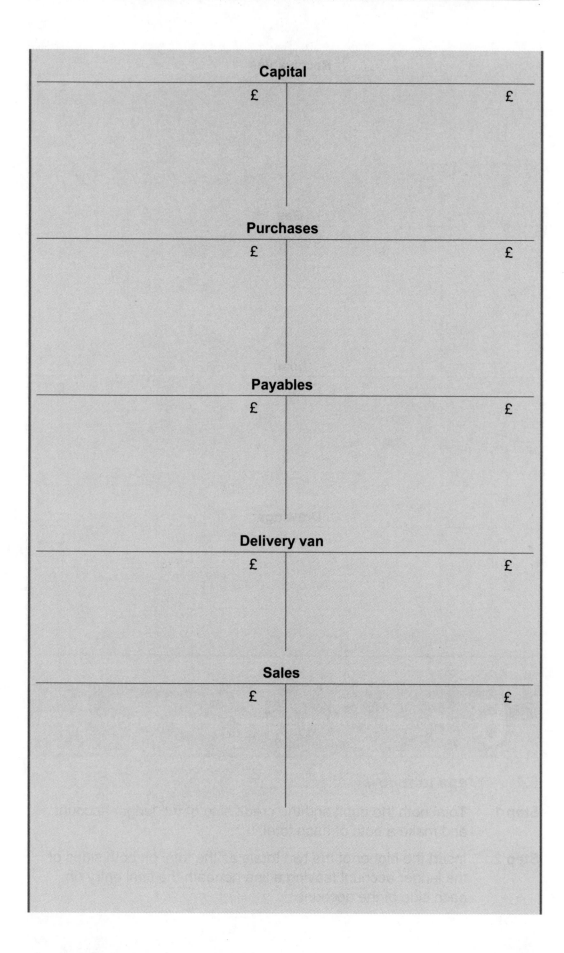

Capital

£		£

Purchases

£		£

Payables

£		£

Delivery van

£		£

Sales

£		£

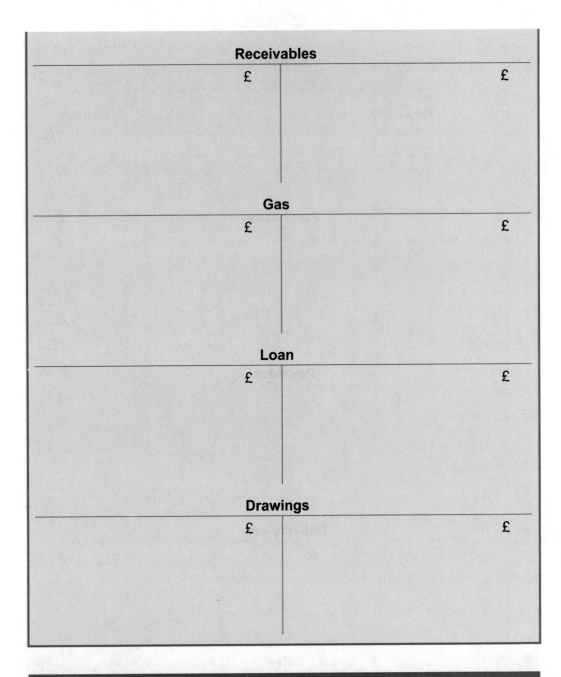

Receivables

£	£

Gas

£	£

Loan

£	£

Drawings

£	£

6 Procedure for balancing a ledger account

6.1 Steps to follow

Step 1 Total both the debit and the credit side of the ledger account and make a note of each total.

Step 2 Insert the higher of the two totals as the total on both sides of the ledger account leaving a line beneath the final entry on each side of the account.

Step 3 On the side with the smaller total insert the figure needed to make this column add up to the total. Call this figure the balance carried down (or 'Bal c/d' as an abbreviation).

Step 4 On the opposite side of the ledger account, below the total insert this same figure and call it the balance brought down (or 'Bal b/d' as an abbreviation).

Example

The bank account of a business has the following entries:

Bank

	£		£
Capital	1,000	Purchases	200
Sales	300	Drawings	100
Sales	400	Rent	400
Capital	500	Stationery	300
Sales	800	Purchases	400

Calculate the balance on the account and bring the balance down as a single amount.

Solution

Step 1 Total both sides of the account and make a note of the totals. (Note that these totals that are asterisked below would not normally be written into the ledger account itself. They are only shown here to explain the process more clearly.)

Bank

	£		£
Capital	1,000	Purchases	200
Sales	300	Drawings	100
Sales	400	Rent	400
Capital	500	Stationery	300
Sales	800	Purchases	400
	-----		-----
*Sub-total debits**	*3,000*	*Sub-total credits**	*1,400*

Step 2   Insert the higher total as the total of both sides.

Bank

	£		£
Capital	1,000	Purchases	200
Sales	300	Drawings	100
Sales	400	Rent	400
Capital	500	Stationery	300
Sales	800	Purchases	400
*Sub-total debits**	*3,000*	*Sub-total credits**	*1,400*
Total	3,000	Total	3,000

Step 3   Insert a balancing figure on the side of the account with the lower sub-total. This is referred to as the 'balance carried down' or 'bal c/d' for short.

Bank

	£		£
Capital	1,000	Purchases	200
Sales	300	Drawings	100
Sales	400	Rent	400
Capital	500	Stationery	300
Sales	800	Purchases	400
*Sub-total debits**	*3,000*	*Sub-total credits**	*1,400*
		Bal c/d	1,600
Total	3,000	Total	3,000

Step 4 Insert the balance carried down figure beneath the total on the other side of the account. This is referred to as 'bal b/d' for short.

Bank

	£		£
Capital	1,000	Purchases	200
Sales	300	Drawings	100
Sales	400	Rent	400
Capital	500	Stationery	300
Sales	800	Purchases	400
	———		———
*Sub-total debits**	*3,000*	*Sub-total credits**	*1,400*
		Bal c/d	1,600
	———		———
Total	3,000	Total	3,000
	———		———
Bal b/d	1,600		

The closing balance carried down at the end of the period is also the opening balance brought down at the start of the next period. This opening balance remains in the account as the starting position and any further transactions are then added into the account. In this case the balance brought down is a debit balance as there is money in the bank account making it an asset.

Example

Consider again the ledger accounts from the earlier example Percy in this chapter which are reproduced below and balance them.

Bank

Date			£	Date			£
1 Jan	Capital	(1)	20,000	1 Jan	Van	(2)	500
5 Jan	Sales	(6)	2,000		Purchases	(3)	1,000
					Drawings	(4)	50
				5 Jan	Purchases	(5)	500
				15 Jan	Rent	(7)	200

Capital

Date			£	Date			£
				1 Jan	Bank	(1)	20,000

Van

Date			£	Date	£
1 Jan	Bank	(2)	500		

Purchases

Date			£	Date	£
1 Jan	Bank	(3)	1,000		
5 Jan	Bank	(5)	500		

Drawings

Date			£	Date	£
1 Jan	Bank	(4)	50		

Sales

Date	£	Date			£
		5 Jan	Bank	(6)	2,000

Rent

Date			£	Date	£
15 Jan	Bank	(7)	200		

Solution

(a)   **The bank account**

Bank

Date		£	Date		£
1 Jan	Capital	20,000	1 Jan	Van	500
5 Jan	Sales	2,000		Purchases	1,000
				Drawings	50
			5 Jan	Purchases	500
			15 Jan	Rent	200

Step 1   Total both the debit and the credit side of the ledger account and make a note of each total – debit side £22,000, credit side £2,250.

Step 2 Insert the higher of the two totals, £22,000, as the total on both sides of the ledger account leaving a line beneath the final entry on each side of the account.

Bank

Date		£	Date		£
1 Jan	Capital	20,000	1 Jan	Van	500
5 Jan	Sales	2,000		Purchases	1,000
				Drawings	50
			5 Jan	Purchases	500
			15 Jan	Rent	200
		———			———
		22,000			22,000
		———			———

Step 3 On the side with the smaller total insert the figure needed to make this column add up to the total. Call this figure the balance carried down (or Bal c/d as an abbreviation).

Step 4 On the opposite side of the ledger account, below the total insert this same figure and call it the balance brought down (or Bal b/d as an abbreviation).

Bank

Date		£	Date		£
1 Jan	Capital	20,000	1 Jan	Van	500
5 Jan	Sales	2,000		Purchases	1,000
				Drawings	50
			5 Jan	Purchases	500
			15 Jan	Rent	200
			31 Jan	Balance c/d	19,750
		———			———
		22,000			22,000
		———			———
1 Feb	Balance b/d	19,750			

This shows that the business has £19,750 left in the bank account at the end of January and therefore also on the first day of February. As the balance that is brought down to start the next period is on the debit side of the account this is known as a debit balance and indicates that this is an asset – money in the bank account.

(b) Capital

Capital

Date	£	Date	£
		1 Jan Bank	20,000

As there is only one entry in this account there is no need to balance the account. The entry is on the credit side and is known as a credit balance. A credit balance is a liability of the business and this account shows that the business owes the owner £20,000 of capital.

(c) Van

Van

Date	£	Date	£
1 Jan Bank	500		

Again, there is no need to balance this account as there is only one entry. This is a debit balance as it is an asset – the non-current asset, the van, which cost £500.

(d) Purchases

Purchases

Date	£	Date	£
1 Jan Bank	1,000		
5 Jan Bank	500	31 Jan Balance c/d	1,500
	1,500		1,500
1 Feb Balance b/d	1,500		

This now shows that during the month £1,500 of purchases was made. This is a debit balance as purchases are an expense of the business.

(e) Drawings

Drawings

Date	£	Date	£
1 Jan Bank	50		

This is a debit balance as drawings are a reduction of the capital owed to the owner which is a credit balance.

(f) **Sales**

Sales

Date	£	Date	£
		5 Jan Bank	2,000

There is no need to balance the account as there is only one entry – a £2,000 credit balance representing income.

(g) **Rent**

Rent

Date	£	Date	£
15 Jan Bank	200		

As there is only one entry there is no need to balance the account. This is a debit balance indicating that there has been an expense of £200 of rent incurred during the month.

Activity 3

Given below is a bank account ledger account for the month of March. You are required to 'balance off' the ledger account.

Bank

Date	£	Date	£
1 Mar Capital	12,000	3 Mar Purchases	3,000
7 Mar Sales	5,000	15 Mar Non-current asset	2,400
19 Mar Sales	2,000	20 Mar Purchases	5,300
22 Mar Sales	3,000	24 Mar Rent	1,000
		28 Mar Drawings	2,000

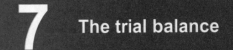

The trial balance

7.1 List of balances

The trial balance is a list showing the balances brought down on each ledger account. An example of a simple trial balance is given below:

	Debit £	Credit £
Sales		5,000
Opening inventory	100	
Purchases	3,000	
Rent	200	
Car	3,000	
Receivables	100	
Payables		1,400
	6,400	6,400

The trial balance is produced immediately after the double entry has been completed and balances extracted on the accounts. If the double entry has been done correctly, the total of the debits will equal the total of the credits.

7.2 Reasons for extracting a trial balance

Drafting a trial balance is a way of ensuring that double entries have been correctly completed.

Example

The following are the balances on the accounts of Ernest at 31 December 20X8.

	£
Sales	47,140
Purchases	26,500
Receivables	7,640
Payables	4,320
General expenses	9,430
Loan	5,000
Plant and machinery at cost	7,300
Motor van at cost	2,650
Drawings	7,500
Rent and rates	6,450
Insurance	1,560
Bank overdraft	2,570
Capital	10,000

Required:

Prepare Ernest's trial balance as at 31 December 20X8.

Solution

Step 1   Set up a blank trial balance

Step 2   Work down the list of balances one by one using what you have learned so far about debits and credits. Assets and expenses are debit balances and liabilities and income are credit balances.

The mnemonic DEAD CLIC may help.

Drs increase:	**Crs increase:**
Expenses	Liabilities
Assets	Income
Drawings	Capital

Trial balance at 31 December 20X8

	Dr £	Cr £
Sales		47,140
Purchases	26,500	
Receivables	7,640	
Payables		4,320
General expenses	9,430	
Loan		5,000
Plant and machinery at cost	7,300	
Motor van at cost	2,650	
Drawings	7,500	
Rent and rates	6,450	
Insurance	1,560	
Bank overdraft		2,570
Capital		10,000
	69,030	69,030

Take care with drawings. These are a reduction of the capital owed back to the owner therefore as a reduction of a liability they must be a debit balance.

The bank overdraft is an amount owed to the bank therefore it must be a credit balance.

Activity 4

Continuing with the example of Percy, complete the trial balance.

8 Summary

In this chapter we have studied cash and credit transactions. It is important to always start with the bank account and remember that cash received is a debit in the bank account and cash paid out is a credit in the bank account. If you get that right then the rest really does fall into place.

You should also be aware of the definitions of assets, expenses and income and the normal entries that you would make in the accounts for these.

Balancing an account is a very important technique which you must be able to master. You must understand how to bring the balance down onto the correct side and what that balance represents.

Answers to chapter activities

Activity 1

The figures in brackets are used here to indicate the transaction number in the activity. They can be used to match the debit entry for the transaction with the corresponding credit entry.

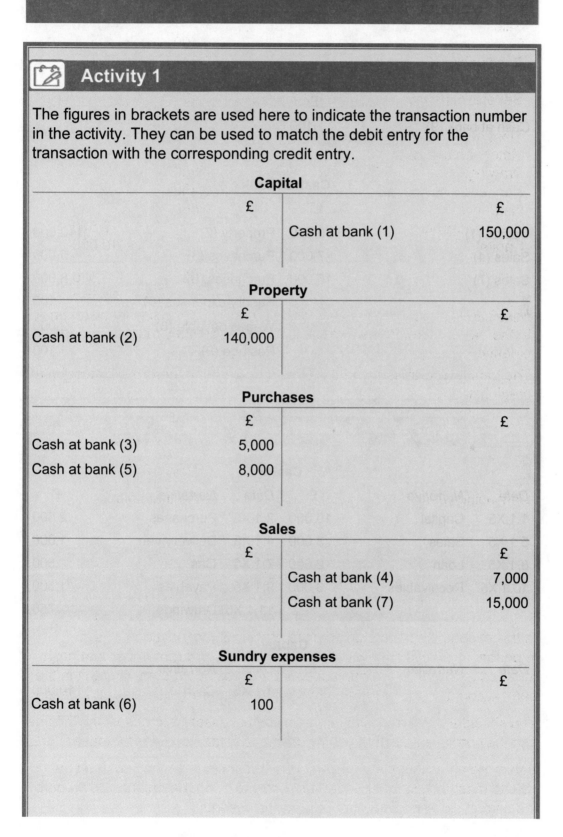

Capital

	£		£
		Cash at bank (1)	150,000

Property

	£		£
Cash at bank (2)	140,000		

Purchases

	£		£
Cash at bank (3)	5,000		
Cash at bank (5)	8,000		

Sales

	£		£
		Cash at bank (4)	7,000
		Cash at bank (7)	15,000

Sundry expenses

	£		£
Cash at bank (6)	100		

Wages expense

	£		£
Cash at bank (8)	2,000		

Postage

	£		£
Cash at bank (9)	100		

Cash at bank

	£		£
Capital (1)	150,000	Property (2)	140,000
Sales (4)	7,000	Purchases (3)	5,000
Sales (7)	15,000	Purchases (5)	8,000
		Sundry expenses (6)	100
		Wages payable (8)	2,000
		Postage (9)	100

Activity 2

Cash

Date	Narrative	£	Date	Narrative	£
1.1.X5	Capital	10,000	2.1.X5	Purchases	2,500
5.1.X5	Sales	3,000	4.1.X5	Delivery van	1,000
8.1.X5	Loan	2,000	7.1.X5	Gas	500
10.1.X5	Receivables	3,000	9.1.X5	Payables	1,500
			11.1.X5	Drawings	750

Capital

Date	Narrative	£	Date	Narrative	£
			1.1.X5	Cash	10,000

Purchases

Date	Narrative	£	Date	Narrative	£
2.1.X5	Cash	2,500			
3.1.X5	Payables	2,000			

Payables

Date	Narrative	£	Date	Narrative	£
9.1.X5	Cash	1,500	3.1.X5	Purchases	2,000

Delivery van

Date	Narrative	£	Date	Narrative	£
4.1.X5	Cash	1,000			

Sales

Date	Narrative	£	Date	Narrative	£
			5.1.X5	Cash	3,000
			6.1.X5	Receivables	5,000

Receivables

Date	Narrative	£	Date	Narrative	£
6.1.X5	Sales	5,000	10.1.X5	Cash	3,000

Gas

Date	Narrative	£	Date	Narrative	£
7.1.X5	Cash	500			

Loan

Date	Narrative	£	Date	Narrative	£
			8.1.X5	Cash	2,000

Drawings

Date	Narrative	£	Date	Narrative	£
11.1.X5	Cash	750			

Activity 3

Bank

Date		£	Date		£
1 Mar	Capital	12,000	3 Mar	Purchases	3,000
7 Mar	Sales	5,000	15 Mar	Non-current asset	2,400
19 Mar	Sales	2,000	20 Mar	Purchases	5,300
22 Mar	Sales	3,000	24 Mar	Rent	1,000
			28 Mar	Drawings	2,000
			31 Mar	Balance c/d	8,300
		22,000			22,000
1 Apr	Balance b/d	8,300			

Activity 4

Trial balance

	Dr £	Cr £
Bank	19,750	
Capital		20,000
Van	500	
Purchases	1,500	
Drawings	50	
Sales		2,000
Rent	200	
	22,000	22,000

9 Test your knowledge

Workbook Activity 5

Z, the owner of a consultancy firm, has the following transactions:

(a) Pays £4,000 into the bank as capital.

(b) Buys a computer for £1,000.

(c) Pays rent of £400.

(d) Earns £800 for consultancy services.

Write up the ledger accounts for the above.

Workbook Activity 6

B makes the following cash transactions:

(a) Pays £4,000 into the bank as capital.

(b) Buys goods for £700.

(c) Buys champagne to entertain the staff for £300.

(d) Purchases three computers for £3,000.

(e) Sells goods for £1,500 cash.

(f) Draws £500 cash.

(g) Purchases goods for £1,200 cash.

(h) Pays telephone bill of £600.

(i) Receives telephone bill rebate of £200.

(j) Buys stationery for £157.

Write up the ledger accounts for the above.

Workbook Activity 7

A sells books to B for £1,000 on credit.

A also sells books to C for £90 credit.

B pays £500 and C pays £90.

Write up these transactions in the sales ledger accounts of A, using individual receivable accounts for each customer.

Workbook Activity 8

The following bank account has been written up for the month of May 20X9. There was no opening balance.

Bank

	£		£
Capital	10,000	Computer	1,000
Sales	2,000	Telephone	567
Sales	3,000	Rent	1,500
Sales	2,000	Rates	125
		Stationery	247
		Petrol	49
		Purchases	2,500
		Drawings	500
		Petrol	42

Bring down the balance on the account.

Workbook Activity 9

The following bank account has been written up during May 20X9. There was no brought forward balance.

Bank

	£		£
Capital	5,000	Purchases	850
Sales	1,000	Fixtures	560
Sales	876	Van	1,500
Rent rebate	560	Rent	1,300
Sales	1,370	Rates	360
		Telephone	220
		Stationery	120
		Petrol	48
		Car repairs	167

Bring down the balance on the account.

Workbook Activity 10

The following bank account has been written up during June 20X9.

Bank

	£		£
Balance b/f	23,700	Drawings	4,000
Sales	2,300	Rent	570
Sales	1,700	Purchases	6,000
Receivables	4,700	Rates	500
		Salaries	3,600
		Car expenses	460
		Petrol	49
		Petrol	38
		Electricity	210
		Stationery	89

Bring down the balance on the account.

Workbook Activity 11

The following are the balances on the accounts of XYZ at 31 August 20X9:

	£
Sales	41,770
Purchases	34,680
Receivables	6,790
Payables	5,650
General expenses	12,760
Loan	10,000
Plant and machinery at cost	5,000
Motor van at cost	6,000
Drawings	2,000
Rent and rates	6,700
Insurance	4,000
Bank overdraft	510
Capital	20,000

Prepare XYZ's trial balance as at 31 August 20X9.

Workbook Activity 12

Tony makes the following transactions during the month of July 20X9:

(a)   Purchases good on credit for £1,000.

(b)   Pays cash for rent of £500.

(c)   Makes sales on credit for £1,500.

(d)   Buys a computer for £900 cash.

(e)   Pays cash for wages of £1,000.

(f)   Receives cash from a credit customer of £400.

(g)   Pays £300 cash to a credit supplier.

(h)   Pays £200 cash for a telephone bill.

(i)   Receives £50 cash refund for overcharge on telephone bill.

(j)   Makes cash purchases of £400.

(k)   Makes cash sales of £2,000.

Write up the ledger accounts for these transactions, balance the accounts off and extract Tony's Trial Balance at 31 July 20X9.

Accounting for credit sales, VAT and discounts

5

Introduction

In this chapter we will consider, in more detail, the effects of discounts and VAT when accounting for credit sales.

KNOWLEDGE

Explain the difference between settlement, trade and bulk discount (3.1)

Describe the effect that settlement discount has on the sales tax (VAT) charged (3.2)

SKILLS

Use source documents to prepare invoices or credit notes (4.1)

Calculate invoice or credit note amounts reflecting any (4.2)

- Trade discount
- Bulk discount
- Settlement discount
- Sales tax (VAT)

CONTENTS

1 Discounts
2 Settlement discount and VAT (sales tax)
3 Accounting for credit sales and VAT (sales tax)

1 Discounts

1.1 Introduction

We have already been introduced to different types of discounts in an earlier chapter but we shall revise them here. There are three main types of discount that a business might offer to its credit customers, a bulk discount, a trade discount and a settlement discount.

1.2 Bulk discounts

A bulk discount is a percentage of the list price of the goods being sold that is deducted from the list price when purchasing large quantities.

1.3 Trade discounts

A trade discount is a percentage of the list price of the goods being sold that is deducted from the list price for certain customers. This discount may be offered due to the fact that the customer is a frequent and valued customer or because the customer is another business rather than an individual.

A trade discount is a definite amount deducted from the list price total of the invoice.

1.4 Settlement discounts

A settlement discount (which may also be referred to as a cash discount) is offered to customers if they settle the invoice within a certain time period. It is up to the customer to decide whether or not to pay early and therefore take the settlement discount. The discount is expressed as a percentage of the invoice total but is not deducted from the invoice total as it is not certain when the invoice is sent out whether or not it will be accepted. Instead the details of the settlement discount will be noted at the bottom of the invoice.

A settlement discount can be offered but it is up to the customer whether or not to take advantage of it.

2 Settlement discount and VAT (sales tax)

2.1 Introduction

When a settlement discount is offered, this makes the VAT calculation slightly more complex.

Invoices should show the VAT payable as 20% (or whichever rate of VAT is applicable) of the **discounted price**. The amount paid by the customer is either:

(a) taking discount – discounted amount (excluding VAT) plus discounted VAT; or

(b) not taking discount – full amount (excluding VAT) plus discounted VAT.

The amount of VAT paid is always based on the discounted amount even though when the invoice is being prepared it is not known whether the customer will or will not take advantage of the cash or settlement discount. Note that if the customer does not pay early to take advantage of the settlement discount, the VAT is not recalculated.

Example

A purchase is for 20 items @ £15 each. This totals £300. A 2% discount is offered for settlement within 30 days.

(a) Calculate the VAT (at 20%).

(b) Calculate the amounts to be invoiced.

Solution

(a) The VAT is therefore calculated as:

300 × 98% = 294

294 × 20% = 58.80

(b) **Invoice amount**

	£
Net	300.00
VAT (part (a))	58.80
Total	358.80

We do not show the discounted amount on the invoice as it is uncertain if the customer will pay within the period required

---

Example

A sales invoice is to be prepared for two adult Fairisle sweaters at a cost of £50.00 each. A settlement discount of 5% for payment within 30 days is offered. What would the sales invoice look like? VAT is at 20%.

Solution

INVOICE

Creative Clothing

3 The Mall, Wanstead, London, E11 3AY,
Tel: 0208 491 3200, Fax: 0208 491 3220

Invoice to:			VAT reg:	487 3921 12
Smith & Isaacs			Date/tax point:	14 February 20X0
23 Sloane Street			Invoice number:	149
London			Delivery note no:	41682
SW3			Account no:	SL43

Code	Description	Quantity	VAT rate %	Unit price (£)	Amount (£)
FW168	Fairisle Sweater (adult)	2	20.00	50.00	100.00
	Total net amount				100.00
	VAT				19.00
	Total amount payable				119.00

Terms: **Deduct discount of 5% if paid within 30 days**

The VAT is calculated at 20% × (£100 × 95%) = £19.

Activity 1

A customer orders 10 Sansui radios priced at £25 each. The customer is given a 20% trade discount and a 10% settlement discount for prompt payment. Calculate the VAT charged on the sale and show the figures to be included on the invoice.

KAPLAN PUBLISHING

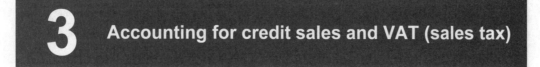

3 Accounting for credit sales and VAT (sales tax)

3.1 Accounting entries

We have already seen in an earlier chapter that a business makes no profit out of any VAT charged on its sales. Instead this amount of output tax (less any related input tax) is paid over to HM Revenue and Customs. Therefore when a credit sale is recorded in the sales account it must be at the net of VAT amount.

However, when our customer eventually pays us he will pay the full amount due, i.e. the gross amount including the VAT. Therefore when we record a receivable in the ledger accounts it must be at the full gross amount of the invoice.

The difference between these two amounts, the VAT, is recorded in the VAT control account.

3.2 Summary of entries

In summary the accounting entries for a credit sale with VAT are:

Debit   Receivables account with the gross amount

Credit   Sales account with the net amount

Credit   VAT control account with the VAT

Work through the following examples to practise the double entry for credit sales.

Example 1

C sells £2,000 of goods net of VAT (at 20%) to Z on credit. He offers Z a 5% settlement discount if Z pays within 30 days. Z does not pay his account within 30 days and so does not take the settlement discount. Z pays after 40 days. Enter these transactions in the accounts.

Solution

Step 1   Calculate the VAT on the sale.

	£
Sales value net of VAT	2,000.00
VAT = (2,000 – 5%) × 20%	380.00
Invoice value	2,380.00

Note: Remember that when a settlement discount is offered, the VAT is calculated on the sales value minus the settlement discount. In this case it turns out that Z does not take the settlement discount but at no stage do we go back to recalculate the VAT.

Step 2   Enter the invoice in the accounts.

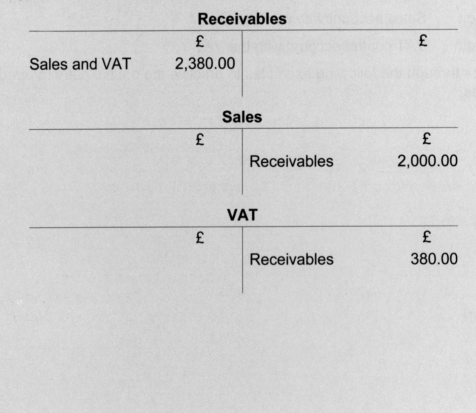

Receivables

	£		£
Sales and VAT	2,380.00		

Sales

	£		£
		Receivables	2,000.00

VAT

	£		£
		Receivables	380.00

Step 3 Enter the payment by Z in the accounts.

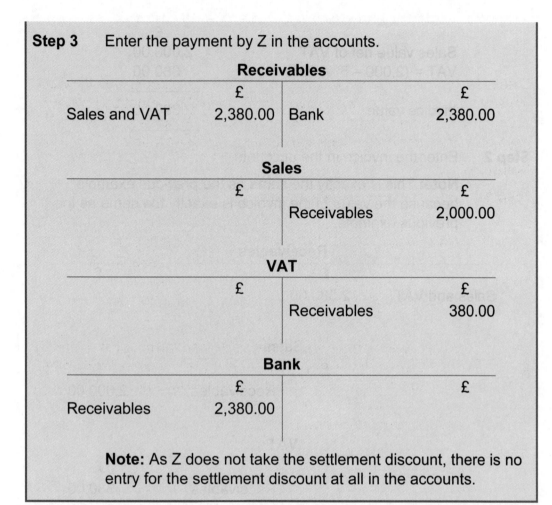

Receivables

	£		£
Sales and VAT	2,380.00	Bank	2,380.00

Sales

	£		£
		Receivables	2,000.00

VAT

	£		£
		Receivables	380.00

Bank

	£		£
Receivables	2,380.00		

Note: As Z does not take the settlement discount, there is no entry for the settlement discount at all in the accounts.

Example 2

Two months later C sells another £2,000 of goods net of VAT at 20% to Z on credit. He offers Z a 5% settlement discount if Z pays within 30 days. This time Z does pay his account within 30 days and takes the settlement discount. Enter these transactions in the accounts.

Solution

Step 1 Calculate the VAT on the sale.

Note: This is exactly the same as the previous example because the calculation of VAT with a settlement discount is the same whether the customer takes the settlement discount or not.

	£
Sales value net of VAT	2,000.00
VAT = (2,000 – 5%) 20%	380.00
Invoice value	2,380.00

Step 2   Enter the invoice in the accounts.

Note: This is exactly the same as the previous example because the value of the invoice is exactly the same as the previous example.

Receivables

	£		£
Sales and VAT	2,380.00		

Sales

	£		£
		Receivables	2,000.00

VAT

	£		£
		Receivables	380.00

Step 3   Calculate the amount paid by Z.

Note: The amount paid by Z will be different from the previous example because Z does take the 5% discount.

	£
Sales value net of VAT	2,000.00
Less: settlement discount = 5% × 2,000	(100.00)
VAT (as per the invoice)	380.00
Amount paid by Z	2,280.00

Step 4   Enter this amount in the accounts.

Receivables

	£		£
Sales and VAT	2,380.00	Bank	2,280.00

Because Z takes the settlement discount, he pays C £100 less than the invoice value. In order to clear the receivables account we have to credit that account with the £100 and debit a discount allowed account with £100. This £100 is an expense of the business as we have allowed our customer to pay less than the invoice value in order to have the benefit of receiving the money earlier.

Sales

	£		£
		Receivables	2,000.00

VAT

	£		£
		Receivables	380.00

Receivables

	£		£
Sales and VAT	2,380.00	Bank	2,280.00
		Discount allowed	100.00

Discount allowed

	£		£
Receivables	100.00		

Bank

	£		£
Receivables	2,280.00		

4 Summary

We have covered some fairly tricky ideas in this chapter and it is very important that you really do understand them.

The calculations of VAT (sales tax) are fairly straightforward but do make sure that you can calculate the VAT element of a sale when you are given the sales value gross of VAT.

Also quite tricky is the treatment of settlement discounts. You have to be able to do two things.

(a) Calculate the VAT on a sale when a settlement discount is offered. Remember that it is irrelevant whether the customer takes the settlement discount or not.

(b) Calculate the amount paid by the customer if he takes a settlement discount. This will be less than the invoice value and you therefore have to account for the discount allowed.

Answers to chapter activities

📝 Activity 1

Note: The answer is arrived at as follows:

(a) **VAT calculation**

	£
Sales price (10 × £25)	250.00
Less: Trade discount (250 × 20%)	(50.00)
	200.00
Less: Settlement discount (200 × 10%)	(20.00)
	180.00
VAT @ 20%	36.00

(b) **Invoiced amount**

	£
Sales value	200.00
VAT	36.00
	236.00

5 Test your knowledge

📝 Workbook Activity 2

Calculate the VAT on the following sales:

(a)   A sale for £140.00 plus VAT

(b)   A sale for £560.00 plus VAT

(c)   A sale for £720.00 including VAT

(d)   A sale for £960.00 including VAT

📝 Workbook Activity 3

Calculate the VAT on the following sales:

(a)   A sale for £280.00 plus VAT where a settlement discount of 2% is offered.

(b)   A sale for £480.00 plus VAT where a settlement discount of 3% is offered.

(c)   A sale for £800.00 plus VAT where a settlement discount of 5% is offered but not taken.

(d)   A sale of £650.00 plus VAT where a settlement discount of 4% is offered but not taken.

📝 Workbook Activity 4

A sells £600 of goods to B. VAT has to be added and A offers B a settlement discount of 3%. Calculate the amount that B will pay A if:

(a)   B takes the settlement discount; and

(b)   B does not take the settlement discount.

Accounting for credit purchases, VAT and discounts

6

Introduction

In this chapter we move on from considering the accounting entries for sales and look here at the equivalent accounting entries for purchases.

KNOWLEDGE

Describe the effect that settlement discount has on the sales tax (VAT) charged (3.2)

SKILLS

Calculate invoice or credit note amounts reflecting any (4.2)

– Trade discount

– Bulk discount

– Settlement discount

– Sales tax (VAT)

CONTENTS

1 Discounts and VAT (sales tax)
2 Credit purchases – double entry

1 Discounts and VAT (sales tax)

1.1 Introduction

We studied discounts and VAT (sales tax) when studying sales. The calculation of VAT and discounts are **exactly** the same when considering purchases. Remember that it is the seller who offers the discounts and it is the seller who charges the VAT, so the fact that we are now studying purchases does not change how these things are calculated.

The purchaser will receive a 'sales invoice' from the seller. This will have details of discounts and VAT exactly as we saw before when studying sales. The purchaser will call this a 'purchase invoice' and enter it in the books accordingly as we shall see.

We shall not therefore go through all the details of VAT and discounts but will simply revise this with a short example.

Example

Carl buys £1,000 of goods from Susan on credit. Susan sends a sales invoice with the goods offering a 5% discount if Carl pays within 30 days. Carl pays within 30 days.

Calculate:

(a)   the VAT

(b)   the total value of the invoice, and

(c)   the amount that Carl will pay.

Solution

(a)   VAT = (£1,000 – (5% × £1,000)) × 20% = £190

(b)   **Total value of invoice**

	£
Goods	1,000.00
VAT	190.00
Invoice value	1,190.00

(c) **Amount Carl will pay**

	£
Goods	1,000.00
Less settlement discount	50.00
	950.00
VAT	190.00
	1,140.00

Note: Remember that if Carl does not pay within 30 days, the VAT is not recalculated – VAT is always calculated at the lowest amount payable, whether the customer takes advantage of the settlement discount or not.

2 Credit purchases – double entry

2.1 Basic double entry

The basic double entry for credit purchases with VAT is as follows:

Debit   Purchases account with the net amount

Debit   VAT account with the VAT

Credit   Payables account with the gross amount

Purchases have been debited with the net amount as the VAT is not a cost to the business. Instead the VAT is an amount that can be set off against the amount of VAT due to HMRC and therefore the VAT is a debit entry in the VAT account. The payables account is credited with the gross amount as this is the amount that must be paid to the supplier.

Work through the following examples to practise the double entry for credit purchases.

Example 1

B sells goods on credit to Y for £500 plus VAT at 20%. Y pays B the full amount due. Record these transactions in the accounts of Y.

Solution

Step 1 Calculate the VAT on the purchase and enter the transaction in the payables, purchases and VAT accounts.

Calculation of VAT

	£
Net value of sale	500.00
VAT at 20%	100.00
Gross value of purchase	600.00

Payables

	£		£
		Purchases and VAT	600.00

Purchases

	£		£
Payables	500.00		

VAT

	£		£
Payables	100.00		

Step 2 Enter £600.00 paid by Y in the payables & the bank account.

Payables

	£		£
Bank	600.00	Purchases and VAT	600.00

Purchases

	£		£
Payables	500.00		

VAT

	£		£
Payables	100.00		

Bank

	£		£
		Payables	600.00

🔆 Example 2

B sells £1,000 of goods to Y net of VAT on credit. He gives Y a deduction of 20% trade discount from the £1,000 net value. Y pays his account in full. Enter these amounts in the accounts of Y.

Solution

Step 1   Calculate the value of the sale net of discount and the VAT at 20% thereon.

	£
Sales value	1,000
Less: 20% discount	200
Net value	800
VAT at 20%	160
Total invoice value	960

Step 2   Enter the invoice in the payables, purchases and VAT accounts.

Payables

	£		£
		Purchases and VAT	960

Purchases

	£		£
Payables	800		

VAT

	£		£
Payables	160		

Note: Note that the trade discount does not feature at all in the accounts. The invoice value is expressed after deduction of the trade discount and it is this invoiced amount that is entered in the accounts.

Step 3 Enter the cash paid by Y.

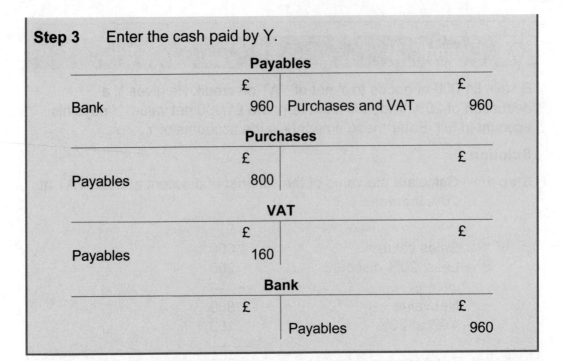

Payables

	£		£
Bank	960	Purchases and VAT	960

Purchases

	£		£
Payables	800		

VAT

	£		£
Payables	160		

Bank

	£		£
		Payables	960

Example 3

C sells £2,000 of goods net of VAT to Z on credit. He offers Z a 5% settlement discount if Z pays within 30 days. Z pays his account within 30 days and takes the settlement discount. Enter these transactions in the accounts of Z.

Solution

Step 1 Calculate the VAT on the purchase.

	£
Invoice value net of VAT	2,000.00
VAT = 20% × (2,000 – (5% × 2,000))	380.00
Invoice value	2,380.00

Step 2 Enter the invoice in the accounts of Z.

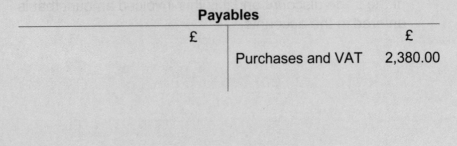

Payables

	£		£
		Purchases and VAT	2,380.00

KAPLAN PUBLISHING

Purchases

	£		£
Payables	2,000.00		

VAT

	£		£
Payables	380.00		

Step 3 Calculate the amount paid by Z.

	£
Invoice value net of VAT	2,000.00
Less: settlement discount = 5% × 2,000	(100.00)
VAT (as per the invoice)	380.00
Amount paid by Z	2,280.00

Step 4 Enter this amount in the accounts.

Payables

	£		£
Bank	2,280.00	Purchases and VAT	2,380.00
Discount received	100.00		

Purchases

	£		£
Payables	2,000.00		

VAT

	£		£
Payables	380.00		

Bank

	£		£
		Payables	2,280.00

Discount received		
£		£
	Payables	100.00

Note: Because Z takes the settlement discount, he pays C £100 less than the invoice value. In order to clear the payables balance we have to debit that account with the £100 and credit a discount received account with £100. This £100 is income (reduction of an expense) of the business as the business is paying less than the face value of the invoice.

3 Summary

The topics covered in this chapter will have been familiar to you as you have already studied the similar topics for sales.

Make sure you understand the point about VAT when there is a settlement discount offered. You must also understand the double entry for settlement discounts.

4 Test your knowledge

Workbook Activity 1

Calculate the VAT for the following:

(a)   X purchases £400 goods from Y net of VAT.

(b)   X purchases £650 goods from Y net of VAT.

(c)   X purchases £528 goods from Y including VAT.

(d)   X purchases £120 goods from Y including VAT.

Workbook Activity 2

Calculate the VAT on the following:

(a)   X purchases £850 goods from Y and takes the 3% settlement discount offered.

(b)   X purchases £600 goods from Y and takes the 5% settlement discount offered.

(c)   X purchases £325 goods from Y and does not take the 2% settlement discount offered.

(d)   X purchases £57 goods from Y and does not take the 4% settlement discount offered.

Workbook Activity 3

Z buys £600 of goods net of VAT from A and takes the 3% settlement discount offered.

Post these transactions in the ledger accounts of Z.

Control accounts and subsidiary ledgers

7

Introduction

We have already seen how credit sales and purchases are recorded into books of prime entry. In this chapter we review how those entries to the day books are entered into the control accounts in the general ledger and into the individual accounts for receivables and payables in the subsidiary sales and purchases ledgers.

KNOWLEDGE
Describe the processing of financial transactions from the books of prime entry into the double entry bookkeeping system (2.4)

SKILLS
Transfer data from the books of prime entry to the ledgers (8.1)

CONTENTS

1 Recording credit sales and purchases
2 The general and subsidiary ledgers
3 Credit sales
4 Sales returns
5 Credit purchases
6 Purchases returns

1 Recording credit sales and purchases

1.1 Introduction

In a typical business there will be a great number of sales and purchases transactions to be recorded. If we were to record each transaction individually, the accounts would get cluttered.

In order to simplify the process (and exercise greater control) we divide the recording of the transactions into three parts.

(a) The first part is the books of prime entry.

(b) The second part is the general ledger itself where the double entry takes place.

(c) The third part is the subsidiary (memorandum) ledgers – individual receivable and payable accounts known as the 'sales ledger' and the 'purchases ledger'. (**Note:** The sales ledger is also sometimes referred to as the subsidiary (sales) ledger and the purchases ledger is also sometimes referred to as the subsidiary (purchases) ledger.)

Invoices, receipts and payments will form the basis of accounting entries in all these three parts.

2 The general and subsidiary ledgers

2.1 Introduction

The general ledger is the place where the double entry takes place in the appropriate ledger accounts. The general ledger contains all the accounts you have become familiar with so far, for example:

Capital

Drawings

Van

Rent

Electricity

Purchases

Bank

etc.

Two of these typical accounts are the receivables and payables accounts but now we will call these the sales ledger control account and the purchases ledger control account.

In the case of the sales ledger control account, this account contains (for a given period) the **total** value of all the invoices issued to customers and the **total** of all the cash received. The purchases ledger control account contains the **total** value of all the invoices received from suppliers and the **total** of all the cash paid. The control accounts do not contain any detail.

[**Note** that the AAT refers to this ledger as the general ledger. In some businesses it is referred to as the 'main ledger' or the 'nominal ledger'. You should be able to use these different terms interchangeably.]

2.2 The sales ledger

As well as information about our receivables in total we have to keep track of each individual receivable. How much have we invoiced him with? What has he paid? How much does he owe?

We do this in the sales ledger. This ledger is not part of the general ledger and it is **not** part of the double entry. (Remember it is also sometimes called the subsidiary (sales) ledger.)

The sales ledger contains a separate ledger account for each individual receivable. Every individual invoice and cash receipt is posted to an individual's account in the sales ledger.

2.3 The purchases ledger

As we require information about individual receivables, the same applies to individual payables. How much have we been invoiced? What have we paid? How much do we owe?

We do this in the purchases ledger. This ledger is not part of the general ledger and it is **not** part of the double entry. (Remember it is sometimes referred to as the subsidiary (purchases) ledger.)

The purchases ledger contains a separate ledger account for each individual payable. Every individual purchase invoice and cash payment is posted to an individual's account in the purchases ledger.

3 Credit sales

We have now looked at the three elements of a typical accounting system. We must now see how it all fits together.

We will first consider three credit sales invoices

Customer	Amount
A	£1,500
B	£2,000
C	£2,500

Step 1

Each invoice is recorded in the sales day book and in the personal account of each receivable in the sales ledger. The entry required for each invoice is a debit in each receivable account to indicate that this is the amount that each one owes us.

Step 2

At the end of the period the sales day book is totalled and the total is entered into the sales ledger control account (SLCA) (total receivables account) in the general ledger.

The full double entry is as we saw in a previous chapter (ignoring VAT at the moment):

Debit   Sales ledger control account

Credit   Sales

Step 3

Now consider the following cheques being received against these debts.

Customer	Amount
A	£1,000
B	£2,000

Each receipt is recorded in the cash book (see later chapter) and in the personal account of each receivable in the sales ledger. The entry for cash received in the individual accounts is a credit entry to indicate that they no longer owe us these amounts.

Step 4

At the end of the period the cash book is totalled and the total is entered into the sales ledger control account (total receivables account) in the general ledger.

The full double entry is:

Debit   Cash account (money in)

Credit   Sales ledger control account

This is illustrated on the next page.

Summary

1   The invoices are entered into the SDB and the cheques are entered into the cash book.

2   The totals from the cash book and SDB are posted to the SLCA.

3   The individual invoices and cash receipts from receivables are posted to the subsidiary sales ledger.

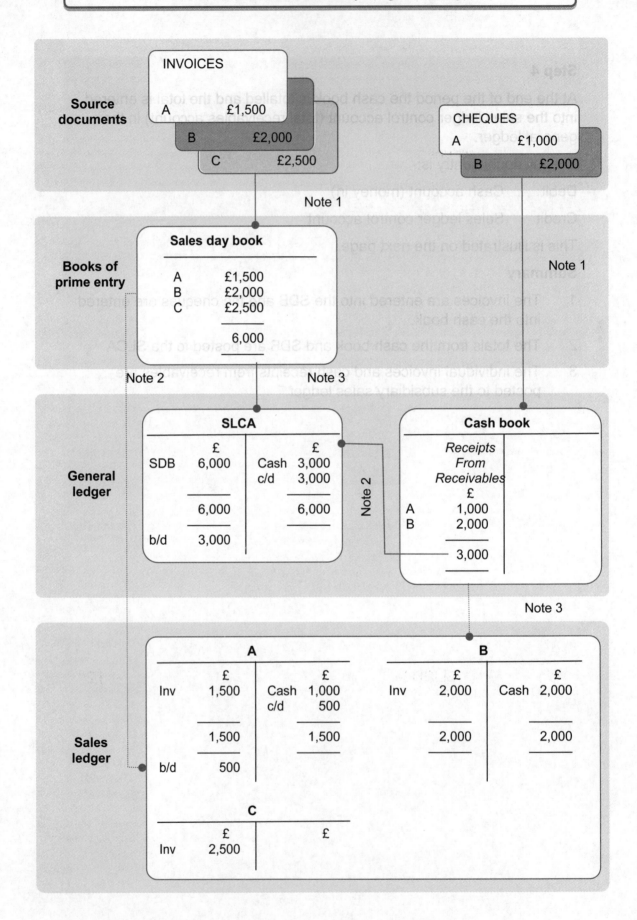

💡 Example

Posting the sales day book to the accounts in the ledgers

Consider the following sales transactions made by Roberts Metals.

Customer	Sales value (ex VAT)	Trade discount	Net sales value	VAT	Total
	£	£	£	£	£
A	1,000	10%	900	180.00	1,080.00
B	2,000	20%	1,600	320.00	1,920.00
C	3,000	30%	2,100	420.00	2,520.00

Enter this information in the ledger accounts using the following three steps.

Step 1   Write up the sales day book, and total the columns.

Step 2   Post the totals to the accounts in the general ledger.

Step 3   Post the individual invoices to the sales ledger.

Solution

Step 1

SALES DAY BOOK						
Date	Customer	Reference	Invoice number	Total £	VAT £	Sales £
	A			1,080.00	180.00	900.00
	B			1,920.00	320.00	1,600.00
	C			2,520.00	420.00	2,100.00
			TOTALS	5,520.00	920.00	4,600.00

Step 2

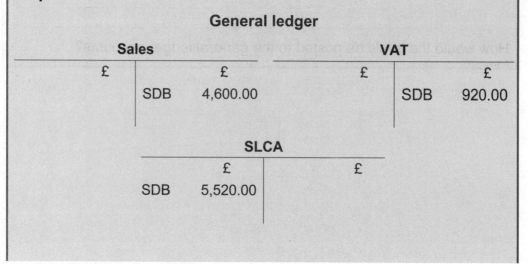

General ledger

Sales				VAT			
£		£		£		£	
		SDB	4,600.00			SDB	920.00

SLCA			
£		£	
SDB	5,520.00		

Step 3

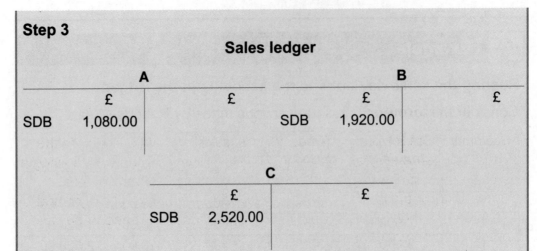

Sales ledger

	A				B	
	£	£			£	£
SDB	1,080.00			SDB	1,920.00	

	C	
	£	£
SDB	2,520.00	

Note to solution

(a)   The totals of the SDB are entered in the general ledger.

(b)   The individual invoices (total value including VAT) are entered in the individual receivables accounts in the sales ledger. This is the amount that the receivable will pay.

(c)   Note that there are no entries for trade discounts either in the SDB or in the ledger accounts.

Activity 1

An analysed sales day book has the following totals for a week.

Date	Invoice no	Customer name	Code	Total	VAT	Europe	Asia	America
				£	£	£	£	£
23/04/X0		Total		65,340	10,890	21,250	15,400	17,800

How would the totals be posted to the general ledger accounts?

---

4 Sales returns

4.1 Introduction

When customers return goods, the accounting system has to record the fact that goods have been returned. If the goods were returned following a cash sale then cash would be repaid to the customer. If goods were returned following a credit sale then the SLCA in the general ledger and the customer's individual account in the sales ledger will need to be credited with the value of the goods returned.

Example

Returns following a cash sale

X sells £500 of goods to A for cash plus £100 VAT

X subsequently agrees that A can return £200 worth of goods (excluding the VAT)

Record these transactions in the ledger accounts.

Solution

Step 1

First of all we need to set up a new account called the 'sales returns account' in the general ledger. This will be used in addition to the sales account and cash book with which you are familiar.

Step 2

Enter the cash sale in the accounts.

Debit bank account for cash received	£600.00
Credit sales with net amount	£500.00
Credit VAT account with VAT	£100.00

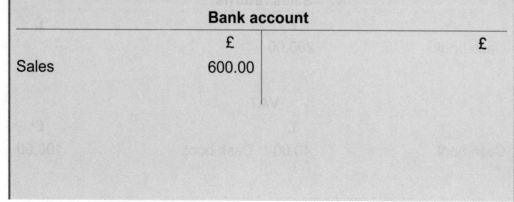

Bank account

	£		£
Sales	600.00		

Sales

	£		£
		Cash book	500.00

Sales returns

	£		£

VAT

	£		£
		Cash book	100.00

Step 3

X will repay A £200 plus VAT of (£200 × 20%) = £40. We therefore need to enter the sale return, the cash and the VAT in the accounts.

Debit sales returns account	£200.00
Debit VAT account £200 × 20%	£40.00
Credit bank account with cash paid out	£240.00

Bank account

	£		£
Sales	600.00	Sales returns	240.00

Sales

	£		£
		Cash book	500.00

Sales returns

	£		£
Cash book	200.00		

VAT

	£		£
Cash book	40.00	Cash book	100.00

4.2 Sales returns for credit sales – no VAT

When a credit customer returns goods, he does not receive cash for the return. Instead the seller will issue a credit note to record the fact that goods have been returned. This credit note is sent to the customer and is entered in the seller's books.

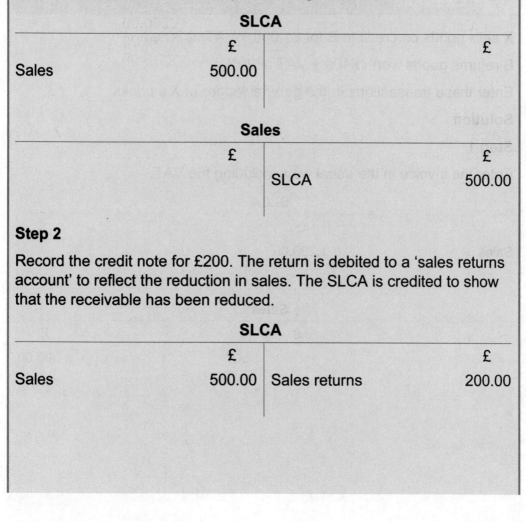

Example

X sells goods on credit to A for £500. A returns goods worth £200. X sends a credit note for £200 to A. Enter these transactions in the general ledger of X's books. There is no VAT.

Solution

Step 1

Record the invoice issued for the credit sale for £500:

Debit the SLCA in the general ledger with £500.

Credit the sales account in the general ledger with £500.

SLCA

	£		£
Sales	500.00		

Sales

	£		£
		SLCA	500.00

Step 2

Record the credit note for £200. The return is debited to a 'sales returns account' to reflect the reduction in sales. The SLCA is credited to show that the receivable has been reduced.

SLCA

	£		£
Sales	500.00	Sales returns	200.00

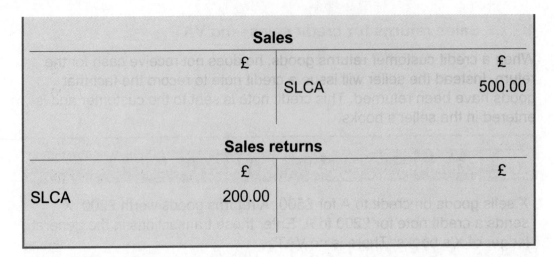

Sales			
	£		£
		SLCA	500.00

Sales returns			
	£		£
SLCA	200.00		

4.3 Sales returns with VAT

When a return is made and we include VAT, the VAT has to be accounted for both on the invoice when the sale is made, and on the credit note when the goods are returned. This VAT has to be entered in the books.

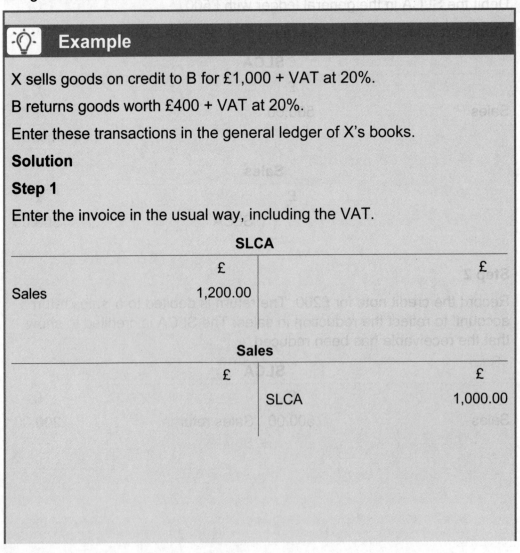

Example

X sells goods on credit to B for £1,000 + VAT at 20%.

B returns goods worth £400 + VAT at 20%.

Enter these transactions in the general ledger of X's books.

Solution

Step 1

Enter the invoice in the usual way, including the VAT.

SLCA			
	£		£
Sales	1,200.00		

Sales			
	£		£
		SLCA	1,000.00

VAT

	£		£
		SLCA	200.00

Step 2

Enter the credit note. The VAT on the return will be £400 × 20% = £80.
SLCA

SLCA

	£		£
Sales	1,200.00	Sales returns	480.00

Sales

	£		£
		SLCA	1,000.00

VAT

	£		£
SLCA	80.00	SLCA	200.00

Sales returns

	£		£
SLCA	400.00		

The books will reflect the position after the return. The balance on the SLCA is £720. This is made up as:

	£
Sale	1,000
Sale return	400
	600
VAT 600 × 20%	120
	720

Example

A and B are credit customers of Ellis Electricals. The balances on their accounts in the sales ledger are £1,200 and £2,400 (VAT inclusive amounts) because both A and B have made earlier purchases which have not yet been paid.

A returns goods which cost £600 excluding VAT. B returns goods which cost £400 excluding VAT.

Enter the above returns in the sales returns day book and in the general and sales ledgers of Ellis Electricals.

Solution

Step 1

Enter the original sales invoices in the general ledger.

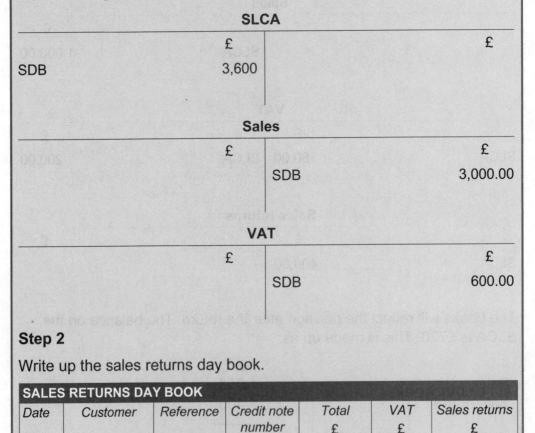

SLCA

	£		£
SDB	3,600		

Sales

	£		£
		SDB	3,000.00

VAT

	£		£
		SDB	600.00

Step 2

Write up the sales returns day book.

SALES RETURNS DAY BOOK						
Date	Customer	Reference	Credit note number	Total £	VAT £	Sales returns £
	A			720.00	120.00	600.00
	B			480.00	80.00	400.00
				1,200.00	200.00	1,000.00

Step 3

Enter the SRDB totals in the general ledger accounts.

SLCA

	£			£
SDB	3,600.00	SRDB		1,200.00

Sales

	£			£
		SDB		3,000.00

VAT

	£			£
SRDB	200.00	SDB		600.00

Sales returns

	£		£
SRDB	1,000.00		

Step 4

Enter the individual amounts in the sales ledger.

A

	£			£
SDB	1,200.00	SRDB		720.00

B

	£			£
SDB	2,400.00	SRDB		480.00

Activity 2

Given below are the totals of an analysed sales returns day book for a week.

Date	Customer name	Credit note no	Code	Total	VAT	Europe	Asia	America
				£	£	£	£	£
23/04/X0				3,360	560	1,458	650	692

Post these totals to the general ledger accounts.

5 Credit purchases

5.1 Introduction

When we studied accounting for sales earlier, we dealt with the three parts of the accounting records as they affected sales.

In the case of purchases, the parts are exactly the same except that instead of a 'sales day book' we have the 'purchases day book', and instead of the sales ledger we have the purchases ledger. The third part, namely the general ledger contains the account for the total payables, the purchases ledger control account (PLCA). Remember that, as for sales, the double entry goes through the general ledger, and the purchases ledger is just a memorandum ledger that holds the details of the individual payable's accounts (it is sometimes called the subsidiary (purchases) ledger).

Below we will illustrate how these parts fit together with a diagram.

5.2 Fitting it all together

Consider these three credit purchases invoices.

Supplier	Amount
X	£4,000
Y	£5,000
Z	£6,000

Step 1

Each invoice is recorded in the purchases day book by the purchaser.

Step 2

At the end of the period the purchases day book is totalled and the total is entered into the purchases ledger control account in the general ledger.

The full double entry is as we saw in a previous chapter (ignoring VAT at the moment):

Debit   Purchases

Credit   Purchases ledger control account

The individual entries are recorded in the individual payable accounts in the purchases ledger.

Now consider these cheques being paid to the payables.

Customer	Amount
X	£2,000
Y	£3,000

Step 3

Each payment is recorded in the cash book.

Step 4

At the end of the period the cash book is totalled and the total is entered into the purchases ledger control account in the general ledger. The individual entries are recorded in the individual payable accounts in the purchases ledger.

This is illustrated below.

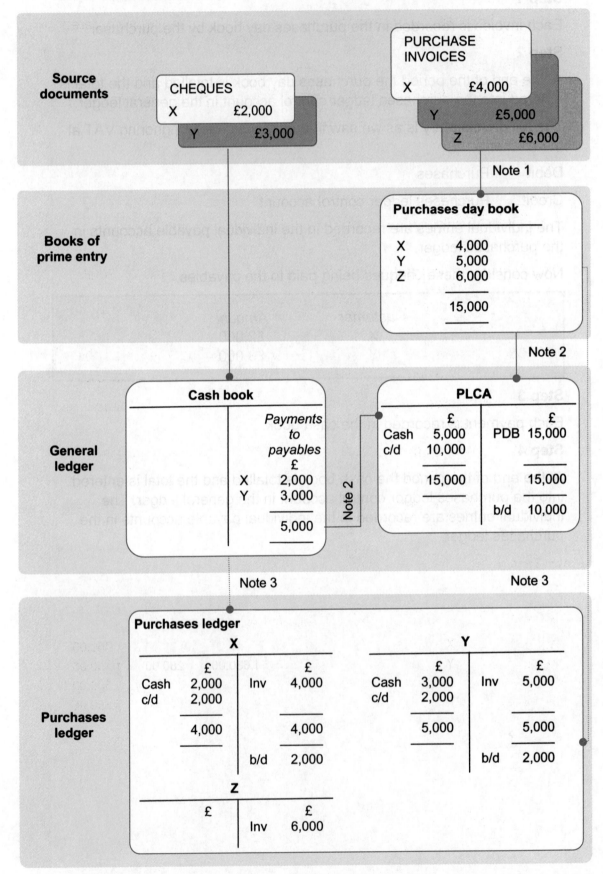

Summary

1   The invoices are entered into the PDB and the cheques are entered into the cash book.

2   The totals from the cash book and PDB are posted to the PLCA.

3   The individual invoices and cash received are posted to the purchases ledger.

Example

Posting the purchases day book to the accounts in the ledgers

Consider the following purchase invoices received from suppliers by Roberts Metals.

Customer	Purchases value (ex VAT)	Trade discount	Net purchases value	VAT	Total
	£	£	£	£	£
X	500	10%	450.00	90.00	540.00
Y	1,750	20%	1,400.00	280.00	1,680.00
Z	5,000	30%	3,500.00	700.00	4,200.00

The following three steps are needed to enter this information in the ledger accounts.

Step 1   Write up the purchases day book, and total the columns.

Step 2   Post the totals to the accounts in the general ledger.

Step 3   Post the individual invoices to the purchases ledger.

Solution

Step 1

PURCHASES DAY BOOK						
Date	Supplier	Reference	Invoice number	Total £	VAT £	Purchases £
	X			540.00	90.00	450.00
	Y			1,680.00	280.00	1,400.00
	Z			4,200.00	700.00	3,500.00
			TOTALS	6,420.00	1,070.00	5,350.00

Step 2

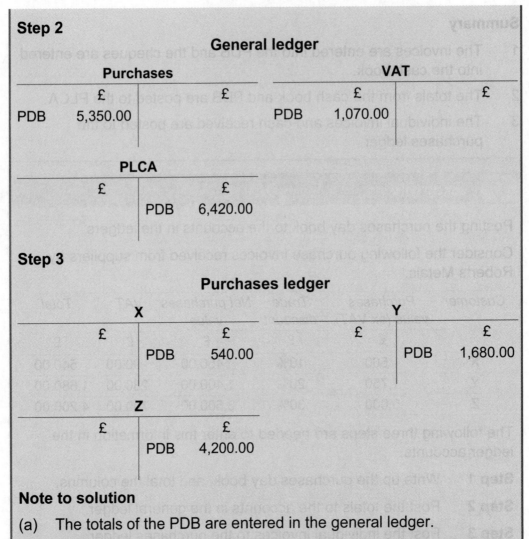

General ledger

Purchases

	£		£
PDB	5,350.00		

VAT

	£		£
		PDB	1,070.00

PLCA

	£		£
		PDB	6,420.00

Step 3

Purchases ledger

X

	£		£
		PDB	540.00

Y

	£		£
		PDB	1,680.00

Z

	£		£
		PDB	4,200.00

Note to solution

(a)   The totals of the PDB are entered in the general ledger.

(b)   The individual invoices (total value including VAT) are entered in the individual payable accounts in the purchases ledger. This is the amount that will be paid to the payable.

(c)   Note that there are no entries for trade discounts either in the PDB or in the ledger accounts.

Activity 3

Date	Invoice no	Supplier	Code	Total	VAT	Dept 1	Dept 2	Dept 3
				£	£	£	£	£
		Total		90,000	15,000	20,000	15,000	40,000

How would the totals be posted to the general ledger accounts?

6 Purchases returns

6.1 Introduction

When a business buys and then returns goods to a supplier, the accounting system has to record the fact that goods have been returned. If the goods were returned following a cash purchase then cash would be repaid by the supplier to the customer who had bought the goods. If goods were returned following a credit purchase then the PLCA in the general ledger will need to be debited and the individual supplier's account in the purchases ledger will need to be debited with the value of the goods returned (we shall see the other entries required below).

Example

Returns following a cash purchase

Y buys £1,000 of goods from B for cash plus £200 VAT (at 20% standard rated)

B subsequently agrees that Y can return £500 worth of goods (excluding VAT).

Record these transactions in the ledger accounts of Y.

Solution

Step 1

First of all we need to set up a new account called the 'purchases returns account' in the general ledger.

Step 2

Enter the cash purchases in the accounts of Y.

Credit cash book for cash paid	£1,200.00
Debit purchases with expense	£1,000.00
Debit VAT account with VAT	£200.00

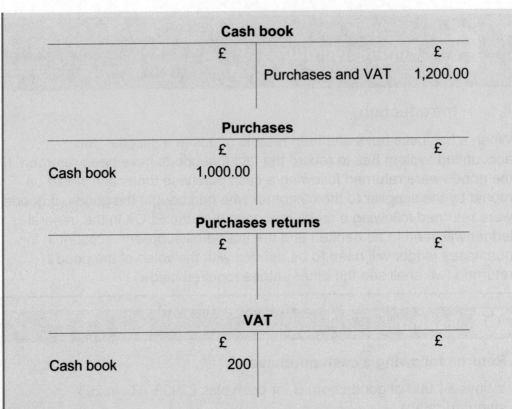

Cash book

	£		£
		Purchases and VAT	1,200.00

Purchases

	£		£
Cash book	1,000.00		

Purchases returns

	£		£

VAT

	£		£
Cash book	200		

Step 3

B will repay Y £500 plus VAT of £100. We therefore need to enter the purchases returns, the cash and the VAT in the accounts.

Cash book

	£		£
Purchases return + VAT	600.00	Purchases and VAT	1,200.00

Purchases

	£		£
Cash book	1,000.00		

Purchases returns

	£		£
		Cash book	500.00

VAT

	£		£
Cash book	200.00	Cash book	100.00

6.2　Purchases returns for credit purchases with VAT

When a credit customer returns goods, he does not receive cash for the return; the seller will issue a credit note to record the fact that goods have been returned. This credit note is sent to the customer and is entered in the customer's books.

When a return is made for goods that incur VAT, we include VAT; the VAT was accounted for on the invoice when the purchase was made, and now has to be accounted for on the credit note when the goods are returned. This VAT has to be entered in the books.

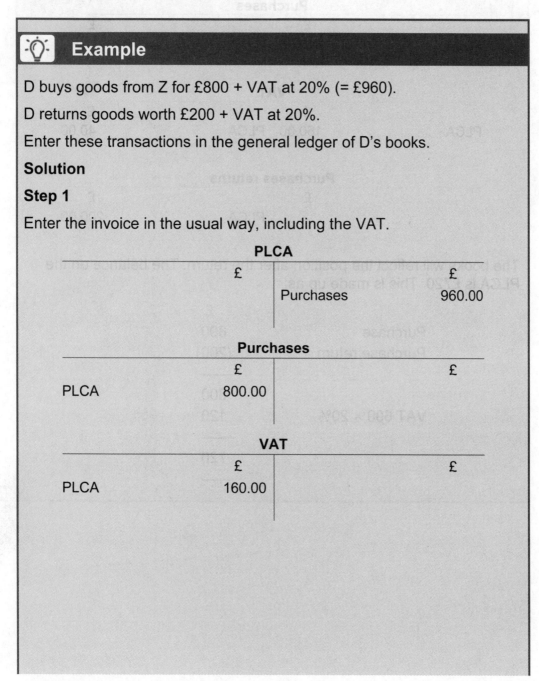

Example

D buys goods from Z for £800 + VAT at 20% (= £960).

D returns goods worth £200 + VAT at 20%.

Enter these transactions in the general ledger of D's books.

Solution

Step 1

Enter the invoice in the usual way, including the VAT.

PLCA

	£		£
		Purchases	960.00

Purchases

	£		£
PLCA	800.00		

VAT

	£		£
PLCA	160.00		

Step 2

Enter the credit note. The VAT on the return will be £200 × 20% = £40.
This gives a total credit note of £240.

PLCA

	£		£
Purchases returns + VAT	240.00	Purchases	960.00

Purchases

	£		£
PLCA	800.00		

VAT

	£		£
PLCA	160.00	PLCA	40.00

Purchases returns

	£		£
		PLCA	200.00

The books will reflect the position after the return. The balance on the
PLCA is £720. This is made up as:

	£
Purchase	800
Purchase return	(200)
	600
VAT 600 × 20%	120
	720

Example

John bought goods for £750 + VAT from X and £1,000 + VAT from Y.

John returns goods which cost £200 excluding VAT to X, and goods which cost £400 excluding VAT to Y.

Enter the above purchases and returns in the general and purchases ledger of John, using a purchases returns day book.

Solution

Step 1

Enter the original purchases invoices in the general ledger.

PLCA

	£		£
		PDB	2,100.00

Purchases

	£		£
PDB	1,750.00		

VAT

	£		£
PDB	350.00		

Step 2

Write up the purchases returns day book.

PURCHASES RETURNS DAY BOOK						
Date	Supplier	Reference	Credit note number	Total £	VAT £	Purchases returns £
	X			240.00	40.00	200.00
	Y			480.00	80.00	400.00
				720.00	120.00	600.00

Step 3

Enter the PRDB totals in the general ledger accounts.

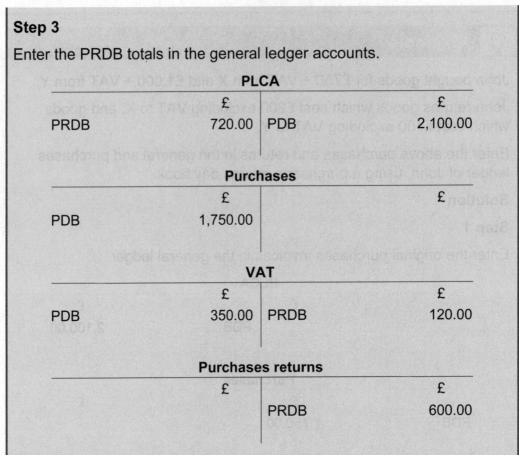

PLCA

	£		£
PRDB	720.00	PDB	2,100.00

Purchases

	£		£
PDB	1,750.00		

VAT

	£		£
PDB	350.00	PRDB	120.00

Purchases returns

	£		£
		PRDB	600.00

Step 4

Enter the individual amounts in the purchases ledger. The amounts will be debited to the individual payable accounts as the return is reducing the amount that is owed to the payable.

X

	£		£
PRDB	240.00	PDB (£750 + VAT)	900.00

Y

	£		£
PRDB	480.00	PDB (£1,000 + VAT)	1,200.00

Activity 4

Given below are the totals of an analysed purchases returns day book for a week.

Date	Supplier	Credit note no	Code	Total	VAT	Dept 1	Dept 2	Dept 3
				£	£	£	£	£
23/04/X0				9,600	1,600	1,000	2,000	5,000

Post these totals to the general ledger accounts.

7 Summary

In this chapter we have reviewed how transactions are recorded.

Initially a transaction is recorded in the relevant book of prime entry (day book).

The double entry takes place in the general ledger, with the total of the gross sales being recorded in a sales ledger control account (SLCA) which we have previously called receivables. The total of the gross purchases is recorded in a purchases ledger control account (PLCA) which we have previously called payables.

Subsidiary sales ledgers contain individual entries for individual receivables whereas the subsidiary purchases ledgers contain individual entries for individual payables.

Answers to chapter activities

Activity 1

The required double entry is as follows:

Debit	Sales ledger control account	£65,340
Credit	VAT	£10,890
	Europe sales	£21,250
	Asia sales	£15,400
	America sales	£17,800

Note carefully that it is the net amount that is credited to each sales account and the gross amount (including VAT) that is debited to the sales ledger control account. The VAT total is credited to the VAT account.

The ledger entries would appear as follows:

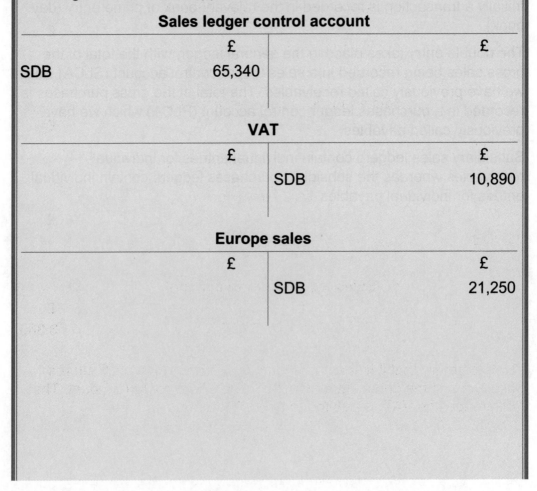

Sales ledger control account

	£		£
SDB	65,340		

VAT

	£		£
		SDB	10,890

Europe sales

	£		£
		SDB	21,250

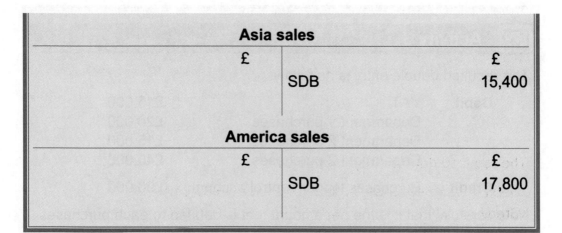

Asia sales

	£		£
		SDB	15,400

America sales

	£		£
		SDB	17,800

Activity 2

Sales returns – Europe account

	£		£
SRDB	1,458		

Sales returns – Asia account

	£		£
SRDB	650		

Sales returns – America account

	£		£
SRDB	692		

VAT account

	£		£
SRDB	560		

Sales ledger control account

	£		£
		SRDB	3,360

Note carefully that it is the net amount that is debited to each returns account and the gross amount to the sales ledger control account. The difference, the VAT, is debited to the VAT account.

Activity 3

The required double entry is as follows:

Debit	VAT	£15,000
	Department 1 purchases	£20,000
	Department 2 purchases	£15,000
	Department 2 purchases	£40,000
Credit	Purchases ledger control account	£90,000

Note carefully that it is the net amount that is debited to each purchases account and the gross amount (including VAT) that is credited to the purchases ledger control account. The VAT total is debited to the VAT account.

The ledger entries would appear as follows:

Purchases ledger control account

	£		£
		PDB	90,000

VAT

	£		£
PDB	15,000		

Department 1 purchases

	£		£
PDB	20,000		

Department 2 purchases

	£		£
PDB	15,000		

Department 3 purchases

	£		£
PDB	40,000		

Activity 4

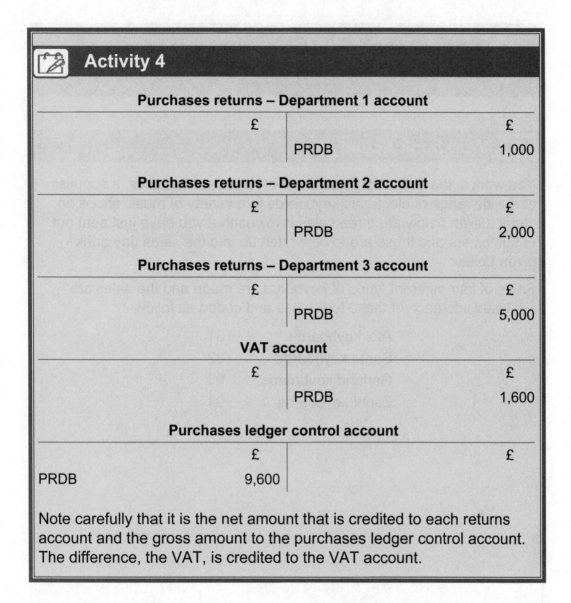

Purchases returns – Department 1 account

	£		£
		PRDB	1,000

Purchases returns – Department 2 account

	£		£
		PRDB	2,000

Purchases returns – Department 3 account

	£		£
		PRDB	5,000

VAT account

	£		£
		PRDB	1,600

Purchases ledger control account

	£		£
PRDB	9,600		

Note carefully that it is the net amount that is credited to each returns account and the gross amount to the purchases ledger control account. The difference, the VAT, is credited to the VAT account.

8 Test your knowledge

Workbook Activity 5

You work in the accounts department of Keyboard Supplies, a supplier of a wide range of electronic keyboards to a variety of music shops on credit. Given below are three sales invoices that you have just sent out to customers and these are to be written up into the sales day book given below.

Sales of four different types of keyboard are made and the sales are analysed into each of these four types and coded as follows:

Atol keyboards	01
Bento keyboards	02
Garland keyboards	03
Zanni keyboards	04

Required:

Write up the analysed sales day book and total each of the columns.

INVOICE

Keyboard Supplies

Invoice to:
BZS Music
42 Westhill
Nutford TN11 3PQ

Trench Park Estate
Fieldham
Sussex TN21 4AF
Tel: 01829 654545
Fax: 01829 654646

Deliver to:
As above

Invoice no:	06116
Tax point:	18 April 20X1
VAT reg no:	466 1128 30
Purchase order no:	77121

Code	Description	Quantity	VAT rate %	Unit price £	Amount excl of VAT £
B4012	Bento Keyboard	3	20	180.00	540.00
Z2060	Zanni Keyboard	6	20	164.00	984.00
					1,524.00
Trade discount 20%					304.80
					1,219.20
VAT					236.52
Total amount payable					1,455.72

Deduct discount of 3% if paid within 10 days, net 30 days

INVOICE
Keyboard Supplies

Invoice to:
M T Retail
Fraser House
Perley TN7 8QT

Trench Park Estate
Fieldham
Sussex TN21 4AF
Tel: 01829 654545
Fax: 01829 654646

Deliver to:
As above

Invoice no:	06117
Tax point:	18 April 20X1
VAT reg :	466 1128 30
Purchase order no:	PO4648

Code	Description	Quantity	VAT rate %	Unit price £	Amount excl of VAT £
A6060	Atol Keyboard	1	20	210.00	210.00
Z4080	Zanni Keyboard	1	20	325.00	325.00
					535.00
VAT					107.00
Total amount payable					642.00

Net 30 days

INVOICE
Keyboard Supplies

Invoice to:
Hammer & Co
1 Acre Street
Nutford TN11 6HA

Trench Park Estate
Fieldham
Sussex TN21 4AF
Tel: 01829 654545
Fax: 01829 654646

Deliver to:
As above

Invoice no:	06118
Tax point:	18 April 20X1
VAT reg :	466 1128 30
Purchase order no:	7486

Code	Description	Quantity	VAT rate %	Unit price £	Amount excl of VAT £
G4326	Garland Keyboard	3	20	98.00	294.00
B2040	Bento Keyboard	5	20	115.00	575.00
					869.00
VAT					168.58
Total amount payable					1,037.58

Deduct discount of 3% if paid within 10 days, net 30 days

Sales day book									
Date	Invoice no	Customer name	Code	Total £	VAT £	01 £	02 £	03 £	04 £

Workbook Activity 6

Graham Haddow runs a buildings maintenance and decorating business and sends out invoices for the work that he has done. He analyses his sales between the maintenance work and decorating work. You are given three sales invoices that he sent out last week.

Required:

Enter the sales invoice details into the analysed sales day book given and total all of the columns.

INVOICE

Graham Haddow

Invoice to:
Portman & Co
Portman House
Tonbridge TN1 4LL

59 East Street
Medford
MF6 7TL
Tel: 0122 280496

Invoice no:	07891
Tax point:	1 May 20X1
VAT reg :	431 7992 06
Your reference:	P2

	Amount excl of VAT £
Repair of window	66.00
Clearing of guttering	73.00
	139.00
VAT	27.24
Total amount payable	166.24

Deduct discount of 2% if paid within 14 days, net 30 days

INVOICE

Graham Haddow

Invoice to:
Stanton Associates
323 Main Road
Tonbridge TN1 6EL

59 East Street
Medford
MF6 7TL
Tel: 0122 280496

Invoice no:	07892
Tax point:	3 May 20X1
VAT reg :	431 7992 06
Your reference:	S3

	Amount excl of VAT £
Decoration of meeting room	1,100.00
VAT	215.60
Total amount payable	1,315.60

Deduct discount of 2% if paid within 14 days, net 30 days

INVOICE

Invoice to:
Boreham Bros
40/54 Hill Drive
Medford MF2 8AT

Graham Haddow
59 East Street
Medford
MF6 7TL
Tel: 0122 280496

Invoice no:	07893
Tax point:	5 May 20X1
VAT reg :	431 7992 06
Your reference:	B7

	Amount excl of VAT £
Repair of door frames	106.00
Re-decorating of door frames	130.00
	236.00
VAT	47.20
Total amount payable	283.20

Sales day book							
Date	Invoice no	Customer name	Code	Total £	VAT £	Maintenance £	Decorating £

Workbook Activity 7

Curtain Decor is a business that makes curtains and blinds to order. Its purchases are analysed between fabric purchases, header tape purchases and others. A separate purchases returns day book is not kept so any credit notes received are recorded as negative amounts in the purchases day book. The business only has five credit suppliers and they are as follows:

Mainstream Fabrics	PL01
C R Thorne	PL02
Fabric Supplies Ltd	PL03
Lillian Fisher	PL04
Headstream & Co	PL05

Today's date is 12 April 20X1 and given below are three invoices and a credit note. These are to be entered into the analysed purchases day book and each column is to be totalled.

INVOICE

Fabric Supplies Ltd

Invoice to:
Curtain Décor
Field House
Warren Lane
Hawkhurst TN23 1AT

12/14 Tike Road
Wadfield
TN11 4ZP
Tel: 01882 467111
Fax: 01882 467112

Deliver to:

As above

Invoice no:	06783
Tax point:	7 April 20X1
VAT reg:	532 6741 09

Code	Description	Quantity	VAT rate %	Unit price £	Amount excl of VAT £
B116-14	Header Tape 14cm	30 m	20	4.62	138.60
P480-G	Fabric – Green	56 m	20	14.25	798.00
					936.60

VAT		183.57
Total amount payable		1,120.17

Deduct discount of 2% if paid within 10 days

INVOICE

Lillian Fisher

Invoice to:
Curtain Décor
Field House
Warren Lane
Hawkhurst TN23 1AT

61 Park Crescent
Hawkhurst
TN23 8GF
Tel: 01868 463501
Fax: 01868 463502

Deliver to:

As above

Invoice no: 0328
Tax point: 7 April 20X1
VAT reg: 469 7153 20

Code	Description	Quantity	VAT rate %	Unit price £	Amount excl of VAT £
TB06	Tie Back Cord – Yellow	10 m	20	6.55	65.50
TB09	Tie Back Cord – Green	4 m	20	6.55	26.20
					91.70
VAT					18.34
Total amount payable					110.04

CREDIT NOTE

Headstream & Co

Credit note to:
Curtain Décor
Field House
Warren Lane
Hawkhurst TN23 1AT

140 Myrtle Place
Fenham
TN16 4SJ
Tel: 01842 303136
Fax: 01842 303137

Credit note no: CN0477
Tax point: 7 April 20X1
VAT reg: 663 4892 77

Code	Description	Quantity	VAT rate %	Unit price £	Amount excl of VAT £
HT479	Header Tape 22 cm	2 m	20	8.30	16.60
CCF614Y	CC Fabric – Yellow	4 m	20	12.85	51.40
					68.00
VAT					13.60
Total credit					81.60

INVOICE

Invoice to:
Curtain Décor
Field House
Warren Lane
Hawkhurst TN23 1AT

Mainstream Fabrics
Tree Tops House
Farm Road
Tonbridge
TN2 4XT
Tel: 01883 214121
Fax: 01883 214122

Deliver to:

As above

Invoice no:	07359
Tax point:	8 April 20X1
VAT reg:	379 4612 04

Code	Description	Quantity	VAT rate %	Unit price £	Amount excl of VAT £
DG4167F	Design Guild Fabric – Fuchsia	23 m	20	13.60	312.80
					312.80
Trade discount 10%					31.28
					281.52

VAT 55.45

Total amount payable 336.97

Deduct discount of 1½% if paid within 14 days

Purchases day book								
Date	Invoice no	Code	Supplier	Total	VAT	Fabric	Header tape	Other

Workbook Activity 8

Kingdon Builders analyse their purchases into wood, bricks and cement, and small consumables such as nails and screws. You are given three purchase invoices, recently received, to enter into the purchases day book given.

An extract from the purchase ledger coding manual is given:

Supplier	Purchase ledger code
JR Ryan & Co	PL08
HT Todd Plc	PL13
Magnum Supplies	PL16

Today's date is 3 May 20X1.

Enter the invoices into the analysed purchases day book and total each of the columns.

INVOICE

Invoice to:
Kingdon Builders
Brecon House
Stamford Road
Manchester
M16 4PL

Magnum Supplies
140/150 Park Estate
Manchester
M20 6EG
Tel: 0161 561 3202
Fax: 0161 561 3200

Deliver to:

As above

Invoice no:	077401
Tax point:	1 May 20X1
VAT reg:	611 4337 90

Code	Description	Quantity	VAT rate %	Unit price £	Amount excl of VAT £
BH47732	House Bricks – Red	400	20	1.24	496.00
					496.00
Trade discount 15%					74.40
					421.60
VAT					82.63
Total amount payable					504.23

Deduct discount of 2% if paid within 10 days

INVOICE

Invoice to:
Kingdon Builders
Brecon House
Stamford Road
Manchester
M16 4PL

J.R. Ryan & Co
59 Parkway
Manchester
M2 6EG
Tel: 0161 560 3392
Fax: 0161 560 5322

Deliver to:

As above

Invoice no:	046193
Tax point:	1 May 20X1
VAT reg:	661 2359 07

Code	Description	Quantity	VAT rate %	Unit price £	Amount excl of VAT £
DGT 472	SDGS Softwood 47 × 225 mm	11.2 m	20	8.44	94.53
NBD021	Oval Wire Nails	7 boxes	20	2.50	17.50
					112.03
Trade discount 10%					11.20
					100.83
VAT					20.16
Total amount payable					120.99

INVOICE

Invoice to:
Kingdon Builders
Brecon House
Stamford Road
Manchester
M16 4PL

HT Todd Plc
30 Longfield Park
Kingsway
M45 2TP
Tel: 0161 511 4666
Fax: 0161 511 4777

Deliver to:

As above

Invoice no: 47823
Tax point: 1 May 20X1
VAT reg: 641 3229 45
Purchase order no: 7211

Code	Description	Quantity	VAT rate %	Unit price £	Amount excl of VAT £
PLY8FU	Plywood Hardboard	16 sheets	20	17.80	284.80
BU611	Ventilator Block	10	20	8.60	86.00
					370.80

VAT   71.93
Total amount payable   442.73
Deduct discount of 3% if paid within 14 days

Purchases day book								
Date	Invoice no	Code	Supplier	Total	VAT	Wood	Bricks/ Cement	Consum- ables

Workbook Activity 9

Kingdon Builders have recently received the three credit notes given. They are to be recorded in the analysed purchases returns day book given.

An extract from the purchase ledger coding manual shows:

Supplier	Purchase ledger code	Settlement discount on original purchase
HT Todd Plc	PL13	3%
BL Lukey Ltd	PL03	2%
Magnum Supplies	PL16	2%

Today's date is 3 May 20X1.

You are required to enter the credit notes into the analysed purchases returns day book and to total each of the columns.

CREDIT NOTE

HT Todd Plc
30 Longfield Park
Kingsway
M45 2TP
Tel: 0161 511 4666
Fax: 0161 511 4777

Credit note to:
Kingdon Builders
Brecon House
Stamford Road
Manchester
M16 4PL

Deliver to:

As above

Credit note no: CN06113
Tax point: 28 April 20X1
VAT reg no: 641 3229 45
Purchase order no: 47792

Code	Description	Quantity	VAT rate %	Unit price £	Amount excl of VAT £
PL432115	Door Lining Set – wood 32 × 115 mm	1	20	30.25	30.25
					30.25
Trade discount 15%					4.54
					25.71
VAT					4.98
Total amount of credit					30.69

CREDIT NOTE

BL Lukey Ltd
The White House
Standing Way
Manchester
M13 6FH
Tel: 0161 560 3140
Fax: 0161 560 6140

Credit note to:
Kingdon Builders
Brecon House
Stamford Road
Manchester
M16 4PL

Deliver to:

As above

Credit note no: 06132
Tax point: 28 April 20X1
VAT reg no: 460 3559 71

Code	Description	Quantity	VAT rate %	Unit price £	Amount excl of VAT £
PLY8FE1	Plywood Hardwood 2440 × 1220 mm	2	20	17.80	35.60
					35.60
VAT					6.97
Total amount of credit					42.57

CREDIT NOTE

Magnum Supplies

Credit note to:
Kingdon Builders
Brecon House
Stamford Road
Manchester
M16 4PL

140/150 Park Estate
Manchester
M20 6EG
Tel: 0161 561 3202
Fax: 0161 561 3200

Credit note no: C4163
Tax point: 30 April 20X1
VAT reg no: 611 4337 90

Deliver to:

As above

Code	Description	Quantity	VAT rate %	Unit price £	Amount excl of VAT £
BU1628	Ventilator Brick	5	20	9.20	46.00
					46.00
Trade discount 15%					6.90
					39.10
VAT					7.66
Total amount of credit					46.76

Purchases returns day book								
Date	Credit note no	Code	Supplier	Total	VAT	Wood	Bricks/ Cement	Consum- ables

Payments and receipts

8

Introduction

We will now consider the procedures and requirements of making and recording payments and receipts including maintaining the cash book and petty cash records.

KNOWLEDGE

Outline the purpose and content of these business documents (1.1)

– Petty cash voucher

– Remittance advice

– Statement of account

List the ways in which customers may pay an organisation and an organisation may pay its suppliers (1.3)

SKILLS

Check the accuracy of receipts from customers against relevant supporting documentation (4.4)

Produce statements of accounts to send to credit customers (4.5)

Reconcile supplier statements to purchase ledger accounts (5.3)

Calculate payments due to suppliers (5.4)

Enter receipts and payment details from relevant primary records into a three column analysed cash book (6.1)

Total and balance the cash book (6.2)

CONTENTS

1   Statements of accounts
2   Receiving and making payments
3   Remittances
4   Recording cash receipts and cash payments
5   The cash book as part of the general ledger
6   Petty cash

Enter petty cash transactions into an analysed petty cash book, accounting for tax where appropriate (7.1)

Total and balance the petty cash book (7.2)

Reconcile the petty cash book with the cash in hand (7.3)

Enter the reimbursement of the petty cash expenditure in the petty cash book using the imprest system (7.4)

Statements of accounts

1.1 Introduction

When sales to a customer are on a credit basis, it is important that there are procedures in place to ensure that the monies outstanding are received promptly.

In practice most customers do not settle their debt after receiving every invoice, as customers can purchase from their suppliers numerous times within a month. Therefore, payment will tend to be made when a statement has been sent by the supplier detailing all the invoices, credit notes and any payments that have occurred within the month. The information contained on the statement will come from the individual receivable's account within the subsidiary sales ledger.

When these statements are sent out and then received by the customer, the customer should compare them to the account they hold for the supplier in their subsidiary purchases ledger.

Once the statement has been reconciled against the customer's own accounting records, the customer will then pay the amount due.

> ### 🔍 Definition
>
> **Receivable (customer) statement**
>
> A statement that shows all the invoices and credit notes that have been sent to a particular credit customer for that month, together with any amounts outstanding from previous months. The statement also details any payments received from credit customers.
>
> **Payable (supplier) statement**
>
> A statement that shows all the invoices and credit notes that have been received from a particular credit supplier for that month, together with any amounts outstanding from previous months. The statement also details any payments sent to the credit supplier.

1.2 Layout of statements

Statements can be prepared in a number of different ways. Some also have remittance advices attached to them in order to encourage early payment.

A remittance advice is a blank document that the customer fills out when making a payment to the supplier. It shows the total payment being made and which invoices (less credit notes) the payment is paying off.

1.3 Preparing a receivables' statement

A receivables' statement will normally be prepared from the information in the receivables' individual account in the sales ledger. Different businesses will use different formats but the basics that must be shown are all invoices, credit notes, payments received and discounts for the period together with usually a running total of the balance.

1.4 Procedure for preparing a statement of account

When preparing a statement for a credit customer, it is important that all details are correct therefore a logical and accurate approach is required.

Step 1   Find the customer's account in the filing system for the sales ledger.

Step 2   Work through the account by date order listing each transaction in turn on the statement – invoices as debits and credit notes, payments and discounts as credits.

Step 3   Return to the start of the statement and calculate the balance at each transaction date to appear in the balance column.

Example

Given below are the sales ledger accounts for two of Nick Brookes' customers. We will start by balancing each account to show the total amount due by each customer.

		Mayer Ltd			SL01
		£			£
03/04	001	189.60	10/04	CN001	50.40
14/04	005	211.20	18/04	CRB	136.30
21/04	007	259.20			
26/04	009	196.80	Balance c/d		670.10
		_____			_____
		856.80			856.80
		_____			_____
Balance b/d		670.10			

		Penken Bros	£				**SL04** £
10/04	004		162.00	17/04	CN002		40.80
24/04	008		171.60	21/04	CRB		115.11
28/04	011		141.60	21/04	CRB – discount		3.03
					Balance c/d		316.26
			475.20				475.20
Balance b/d			316.26				

We can now use this information to prepare statements for these two customers as at the end of April 20X2.

Solution

	NICK BROOKES
	225 School Lane
	Weymouth
To: Mayer Ltd	Dorset WE36 5NR
	Tel: 0149 29381
	Fax: 0149 29382
	Date: 30/04/X2

STATEMENT				
Date	Transaction	Debit £	Credit £	Balance £
03/04	INV001	189.60		189.60
10/04	CN001		50.40	139.20
14/04	INV005	211.20		350.40
18/04	Payment		136.30	214.10
21/04	INV007	259.20		473.30
26/04	INV009	196.80		670.10

**May we remind you that our credit terms are 30 days
With 3% discount for payment within 14 days**

NICK BROOKES
225 School Lane
Weymouth
Dorset WE36 5NR
Tel: 0149 29381
Fax: 0149 29382
Date: 30/04/X2

To: Penken Bros

STATEMENT

Date	Transaction	Debit £	Credit £	Balance £
10/04	INV004	162.00		162.00
17/04	CN002		40.80	121.20
21/04	Payment		115.11	
21/04	Discount		3.03	3.06
24/04	INV008	171.60		174.66
28/04	INV011	141.60		316.26

**May we remind you that our credit terms are 30 days
With 3% discount for payment within 14 days**

These are documents that are being sent to customers; therefore it is extremely important that it is completely accurate. Always check your figures and additions.

Activity 1

You are to prepare a statement to be sent out to one customer, Jack Johnson, for the month of May 20X6. At the start of May this customer did not owe your business, Thames Traders, any money. The sales ledger account for Jack for the month of May is given below.

Jack Johnson

Date		£	Date		£
03 May	Invoice 1848	38.79	08 May	Credit note 446	12.40
07 May	Invoice 1863	50.70	15 May	Cash receipt	77.09
10 May	Invoice 1870	80.52	24 May	Credit note 458	16.50
18 May	Invoice 1881	42.40			
23 May	Invoice 1892	61.20			
30 May	Invoice 1904	27.65			

You are required to prepare a statement for Jack on the blank statement given below.

		Thames Traders		
To:	Date:			

STATEMENT				
Date	*Transaction*	*Debit* £	*Credit* £	*Balance* £
May we remind you that our credit terms are 30 days				

1.5 Checking suppliers' statements

We will now consider the perspective of the business receiving a supplier statement. Before any payments are made it is important to check that the supplier's statement is correct. Each invoice and credit note should be checked either to the original documentation or to the supplier's account in the purchases ledger.

When the accuracy of the statement has been ascertained then it must be determined exactly which invoices from the statement are to be paid.

Example

Given below is a statement from a supplier together with that supplier's account from the purchases ledger.

To: Scott Brothers 34 Festival Way Oldham OL2 3BD	Nemo Limited Date: 31 August 20X3

STATEMENT					
Date	Transaction	Total £	Current £	30+ £	60+ £
12 May 20X3	Invoice 2569	92.35			92.35
13 June 20X3	CN 2659	(23.60)			(23.60)
09 July 20X3	Invoice 2701	102.69		102.69	
18 July 20X3	Invoice 2753	133.81		133.81	
02 Aug 20X3	Invoice 2889	56.50	56.50		
10 Aug 20X3	Invoice 2901	230.20	230.20		
28 Aug 20X3	Invoice 3114	243.24	243.24		
	TOTALS	835.19	529.94	236.50	68.75

May we remind you our credit terms are 30 days

Nemo Ltd				
		£		£
13 June CN 2659	23.60		12 May Invoice 2569	92.35
			09 July Invoice 2701	102.69
			18 July Invoice 2753	133.81
			02 Aug Invoice 2889	56.50
			10 Aug Invoice 2901	203.20
			28 Aug Invoice 3114	243.24

To check that the supplier's statement is correct prior to paying any amounts, the statement should be carefully checked to the supplier's account in the purchases ledger.

Solution

The invoice dated 10 August is in the purchases ledger at a total of £203.20 whereas it appears on the supplier's statement as £230.20.

The purchase invoice itself should be accessed from the filing system to determine whether the amount is £203.20 or £230.20. If the supplier's statement is incorrect then a polite telephone call should be made or letter sent to the supplier, Nemo Ltd, explaining the problem.

1.6 Which invoices to pay

Once the supplier's statement has been checked for accuracy then it has to be decided which invoices shall be paid. Most organisations will have a policy regarding the payment of supplier's invoices or, alternatively, a fairly senior figure in the business will decide each month which invoices are to be paid.

 **Example**

Using the supplier's statement shown above suppose that payment has been authorised for all amounts that have been outstanding for 30 days or more. What amount should the cheque be made out for?

Solution

	£
60+ days total	68.75
30+ days total	236.50
Cheque amount	305.25

---

2 Receiving and making payments

2.1 Introduction

Different types of business will receive money from their customers and pay money to their suppliers in different forms.

Examples of different payment types are:

- Cash
- Credit/debit card
- Standing order
- Direct debit
- Cheque

3 Remittances

3.1 Introduction

When a customer pays by cheque for a credit sale, they will also send a remittance advice to detail the invoices that are being paid.

3.2 Remittance lists

All cash received should be listed on a **remittance list** by the supplier (sometimes known as a **cheques received list).**The list should give details of:

- the customer

- the invoice numbers to which the payment relates (if known)

- the amount paid, and

- any discount allowed (see later in this chapter).

The list should be totalled and signed.

3.3   Using remittance advices

When a business issues an invoice to a customer, the invoice will often have a detachable slip. This slip is called a **remittance advice.**

This **remittance advice** is a slip returned by the customer when paying an invoice so as to identify what the payment is for. This makes it much easier for the business receiving the cheque to know which outstanding invoices are actually being paid.

REMITTANCE ADVICE	

Name and address of business the cheque is being sent to

Name and address of business sending cheque

To:

A.J. Broom & Company Limited
59 Parkway
Manchester
M2 6EG

Company name:	Trail Blazers
Address:	Mount House
	West Street
	Manchester
	M4 7F

VAT registration number of business sending cheque

Tel:	0161 484 6490
Fax:	0161 484 6491
VAT reg no:	32141108
Date:	15 Sept X3

Date	Your ref	Amount £	Discount taken £	Paid £
15 Aug X3	68204	618.40	30.92	587.48
20 Aug X3	68210	426.94	21.34	405.60

Invoice amounts being paid

Cheque total

Total paid	£993.08

Cheque number

Cheque no	041261

When receiving cheques from a customer it is vital to ensure that the correct amount has been paid. This can be done by agreeing the amount of the cheque to the details on the remittance advice and to the invoices themselves.

Activity 2

A remittance advice is a document sent by a supplier to a customer to advise the customer that goods ordered have been sent off to the customer. True/False

Example

This morning the following cheques and supporting remittance advices were received in the post by your organisation, A. J. Broom & Company Ltd.

You are required to check the remittance advice and cheque amounts to the invoices given to ensure that the correct amount has been received.

WESTERN BANK 21 High Street Bristol BS1 4TZ	◯	20 – 16 – 80 *14 Sept* 20 *X3*
Pay *A.J. Broom & Company*	Account Payee	or order
Two Thousand and nine pounds		*£2,009.04*
And 4 pence		
		P Smithson PATRICK CARPENTERS
046178	20–16–80	41643121

CENTRAL BANK
52 Warwick Road
Birmingham
B13 4XT

40 – 18 – 30

15 Sept 20 X3

Pay A.J. Broom & Company   or order

One thousand two hundred and

Twenty eight pounds and 74 pence

£1,228.74

Account Payee

J P Roberts

ROBERTS CONSTRUCTION

020106   40–18–30   31164992

REMITTANCE ADVICE

To:	Company name: Address:	Patrick Carpenters Simba Industrial Est. Leeds
A.J. Broom & Company Limited 59 Parkway Manchester M2 6EG	Tel: Fax: VAT reg: Date:	0714 304 2990 0714 304 2963 318 4861 27 14 Sept 20X3

Date	Your ref	Amount	Discount taken	Paid
		£	£	£
23 Aug	68229	1,649.04	–	1,649.04
23 Aug	3217	(360.00)	–	(360.00)
4 Sept	68237	720.00	–	720.00
			Total paid	£ 2,009.04
			Cheque no	046178

REMITTANCE ADVICE

To: A.J. Broom & Company Limited 59 Parkway Manchester M2 6EG	Company name: Address: Tel: Fax: VAT reg: Date:	Roberts Construction Chillian Park Oldham 0201 632 497 0201 632 498 331 4986 91 15 Sept 20X3

Date	Your ref	Amount £	Discount taken £	Paid £
23 Aug	68230	1,228.74	–	1,228.74
			Total paid	£ 1,228.74
			Cheque no	020106

Invoice 68229

A.J. Broom & Company Limited

	59 Parkway	
	Manchester	
	M2 6EG	
	Tel: 0161 560 3392	
Patrick Carpenters	Fax: 0161 560 5322	
Samba Industrial Estate	Tax Point:	23 August 20X3
Leeds	VAT reg:	452 4585 48

Code	Supply	Description	Quantity	VAT rate %	Unit price £	Amount excl of VAT £
336 BTB	Sale	Roof tiles – black	10	20	123.00	1,230.00
667 LL5	Sale	Softwood plank – 20 cm	14	20	10.30	144.20
						1,374.20
VAT						274.84
Total amount payable						**1,649.04**

Invoice 68237

A.J. Broom & Company Limited

59 Parkway
Manchester
M2 6EG

Tel: 0161 560 3392
Fax: 0161 560 5322

Patrick Carpenters
Samba Industrial Estate
Leeds

| | | Tax Point: | 4 September 20X3 |
| | | VAT reg : | 452 4585 48 |

Code	Supply	Description	Quantity	VAT rate %	Unit price £	Amount excl of VAT £
630 CC4	Sale	Oak veneer in Panels	3	20	200.00	600.00
VAT						120.00
Total amount payable						**720.00**

Credit note 3217

A.J. Broom & Company Limited

59 Parkway
Manchester
M2 6EG

Tel: 0161 560 3392
Fax: 0161 560 5322

Patrick Carpenters
Samba Industrial Estate
Leeds

| | | Tax Point: | 23 August 20X3 |
| | | VAT reg: | 452 4585 48 |

Code	Supply	Description	Quantity	VAT rate %	Unit price £	Amount excl of VAT £
950 BB3	Return	Cotswold bricks	1	20	300.00	300.00
VAT						60.00
Total amount credited						**360.00**

						Invoice 68230
		A.J. Broom & Company Limited				
		59 Parkway				
		Manchester				
		M2 6EG				
		Tel: 0161 560 3392				
Roberts Construction		Fax: 0161 560 5322				
Chillian Park		Tax Point:		23 August 20X3		
Oldham		VAT reg no:		452 4585 48		

Code	Supply	Description	Quantity	VAT rate	Unit price	Amount excl of VAT
				%	£	£
160 TT7	Sale	Insulation	5	20	95.50	477.50
632 BS4	Sale	Brick tiles	20	20	33.25	665.00
						1,142.50
Trade discount 4%						45.70
						1,096.80
VAT						219.36
Total amount payable						**1,316.16**

Solution

From Patrick Carpenters

	£
Invoice number 68229	1,649.04
Invoice number 68237	720.00
Credit note 3217	(360.00)
	2,009.04

This agrees with the cheque.

From Roberts Construction

Invoice number 68230	£1,316.16

This does not agree with the cheque as the cheque is made out for £1,228.74. This discrepancy should be brought to the attention of the manager responsible for credit control at Roberts Construction and a polite letter should be written to the customer explaining the error that has been made. Request can be made for payment but if this is a regular customer then the additional amount may simply be added to the next cheque that Roberts Construction sends.

3.4 Payments received with no accompanying remittance advice

If a payment from a customer is received with no remittance advice or other confirmation of which invoices are being paid then it will be necessary to examine the details of this customer's transactions in the sales ledger.

The individual account for this receivable must be extracted from the subsidiary ledger in an attempt to match the payment received to invoices and credit notes.

 Example

A cheque has been received in the post this morning from A J Holland, a credit customer, for £878.00 but it is not supported by any other documentation.

The individual receivable account for A J Holland has been found in the sales ledger.

A J Holland

	£		£
13/05/X2 Invoice 2256	336.67	20/05/X2 Credit 249	54.09
18/05/X2 Invoice 2271	846.23		
20/05/X2 Invoice 2280	447.69		
25/05/X2 Invoice 2288	147.73		

Solution

By a process of trial and error it can be discovered that the invoices that are being paid off are number 2256, 2280 and 2288 less the credit note. It would appear therefore that the cheque is for the correct amount although there might be some concern as to why invoice 2271 has not been paid; maybe there is some dispute over the amount of this invoice which should be investigated.

Always check figures carefully as such errors are often easy to miss.

3.5 Checking cheques

When cheques are received in the post it is important that they are checked for their validity, particularly in respect of:

- the date: a cheque can become out of date as it is only valid for 6 months from the date of issue

- the payee's name: should the same as the one shown on the account the cheque is being paid into

- the words and figures agree; if they disagree the cheque should be return by the bank for amendment or for a new cheque to be issued

- the cheque is signed.

Activity 3

(a) Today is the 15 March 20X3. Would the cheque below be accepted for payment if it were now presented to the National Bank plc?

(b) Give two reasons for your answer.

NATIONAL BANK PLC	**NB**	19 – 14 – 60
18 Coventry Road		
Birmingham		14/8 20 X2

Pay Music World Limited		or order
Ten thousand and twenty pounds 42p		£1,020.42
23 pence		**P DUNSTER**

200550   19-14-60   50732247

---

4   Recording cash receipts and cash payments

4.1   The cash book

Definition

A cash book is a record of cash receipts and payments that conforms to the double entry system.

An analysed cash book is a cash book with additional columns for analysing principal sources and payments for cash.

KAPLAN PUBLISHING

4.2 Recording cash receipts

🔅 Example

The following is an example of the general and sales ledgers, including entries from the sales and sales returns day books.

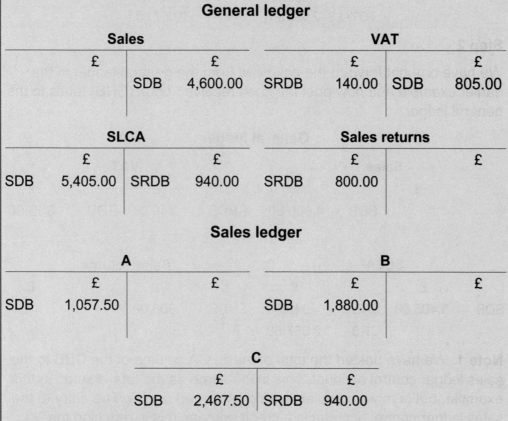

General ledger

Sales

£		£
	SDB 4,600.00	SRDB 140.00

VAT

£	£
SDB	805.00

SLCA

£		£
SDB 5,405.00	SRDB 940.00	

Sales returns

£	£
SRDB 800.00	

Sales ledger

A

£	£
SDB 1,057.50	

B

£	£
SDB 1,880.00	

C

£	£
SDB 2,467.50	SRDB 940.00

The following transactions took place:

Receivable A pays £1,057.50

Receivable B pays £1,000.00

Enter this information in the cash receipts book and in the ledger accounts given above.

Solution

The following steps are needed.

Step 1 Enter these transactions in the cash book.

Step 2 Total the cash book and post the totals to the general ledger.

Step 3 Post the individual amounts of cash paid by receivables to the individual accounts in the sales ledger.

Step 1

CASH RECEIPTS BOOK							
Date	Narrative	Reference	Total	VAT	SLCA	Cash sales	Discount allowed
			£	£	£	£	£
	A		1,057.50	See Note 2	1,057.50		
	B		1,000.00	of Step 2	1,000.00		
		TOTALS	2,057.50		2,057.50		

Step 2

We have brought forward the balances from the general ledger in the earlier example and now post the cash received book (CRB) totals to the general ledger.

General ledger

Sales				VAT			
	£		£		£		£
		SDB	4,600.00	SRDB	140.00	SDB	805.00

SLCA				Sales returns			
	£		£		£		£
SDB	5,405.00	SRDB	940.00	SRDB	800.00		
		CRB	2,057.50				

Note 1: We have posted the total of the SLCA column of the CRB to the sales ledger control account. This is the same as the total column in this example, but in more complex examples it need not be. The entry to the sales ledger control account is a credit entry as this is reducing the amount owed by our receivables.

Note 2: A common confusion is for people to wonder about the VAT – surely some of the money paid by A and B is actually paying the VAT part of the invoice. Yes it is, but we have already accounted for this VAT element when we entered the invoices themselves into the ledger accounts via the sales day book.

The total of the invoices in the SDB were debited to the SLCA and the VAT and sales were the corresponding credits. We therefore now post the total cash including VAT to the sales ledger control account but nothing is posted to the VAT account as this has already been done when dealing with the invoices.

Note 3: This is now the full double entry for the cash received completed.

Debit   Bank account (cash receipts book)

Credit   Sales ledger control account

We have credited the sales ledger control account and the entry in the cash receipts book itself is the related debit entry. So there is no need for any further debit entry.

Step 3

We have brought forward the balance from the sales ledger in the earlier example and now post the cash received to the individual sales ledger accounts. Again, as with the sales ledger control account, this is a credit entry in each case as the cash received is reducing the amount owed by each receivable.

A				B		
	£		£		£		£
b/d	1,057.50	CRB	1,057.50	b/d	1,880.00	CRB	1,000.00

C			
	£		£
b/d	2,467.50	SRDB	940.00

4.3   Settlement discounts allowed to customers

Settlement discounts are a small but tricky complication when dealing with the analysed sales day book and cash book.

We shall consider the same example as before with only one change – receivable A is offered an additional 5% settlement discount if he pays his invoice within 30 days.

Example

The sales day book with settlement discounts

Consider the following sales transactions made by Roberts Metals.

Customer	Sales value (ex VAT)	Trade discount	Net sales value	VAT	Total
	£	£	£	£	£
A	1,000	10%	900	180.00	1,080.00
B	2,000	20%	1,600	320.00	1,920.00
C	3,000	30%	2,100	420.00	2,520.00

In addition to the trade discount, customer A has been offered an additional 5% discount if he pays his invoice within 30 days.

Enter this information in the sales day book and ledger accounts.

Solution

The following steps are needed.

Step 1   Write up the sales day book.

Step 2   Post the totals to the accounts in the general ledger.

Step 3   Post the individual invoices to the sales ledger.

The solution is the same as before except that the VAT for customer A has been recalculated to take account of the settlement discount (W1).

SALES DAY BOOK						
Date	Customer	Reference	Invoice number	Total £	VAT £	Sales £
	A			1,071.00	171.00(W1)	900.00
	B			1,920.00	320.00	1,600.00
	C			2,520.00	420.00	2,100.00
			TOTALS	5,511.00	911.00	4,600.00

Working 1:

	£
Sales value	1,000.00
Trade discount	(100.00)
Net sale value	900.00
VAT (900 – 5%) × 20%	171.00
	1,071.00

Step 2

Enter cash received in the CRB.

CASH RECEIPTS BOOK							
Date	Narrative	Reference	Total	VAT	SLCA	Cash sales	Discount allowed
			£	£	£	£	£
	A		1,026.00		1,026.00		45.00
	B		1,000.00		1,000.00		
		TOTALS	2,026.00		2,026.00		45.00

Note: The CRB does not 'cross-cast', i.e. if you add the totals across (receivables + discounts) this does not equal the total column.

The discount allowed column is known as a 'memorandum column' – it is not really part of the cash book – it is simply there to remind the book-keeper to make an entry in the general ledger as we shall see below.

Step 3 – Posting the CRB totals

The CRB totals are posted as follows to the general ledger.

Sales				VAT			
	£		£		£		£
		SDB	4,600.00			SDB	911.00

SLCA				Discount allowed			
	£		£		£		£
SDB	5,511.00	CRB	2,026.00	CRB	45.00		
		CRB	45.00				

Note that the discount allowed figure in the CRB is entered in the SLCA (to acknowledge the fact that discount has been taken) and is debited to the discount allowed account.

This debit is an expense of the business – allowing the discount has cost the business £45.

Step 4 – Posting to the sales ledger

	A				**B**		
	£		£		£		£
SDB	1,071.00	CRB	1,026.00	SDB	1,920.00	CRB	1,000.00
		Disc	45.00			c/d	920.00
	1,071.00		1,071.00		1,920.00		1,920.00
				b/d	920.00		

	C		
	£		£
SDB	2,520.00		

Note again that the discount is credited to the account of A to show that he has taken the £45 discount which clears his account.

Note also that there is no corresponding debit entry of £45 to a discount account in the sales ledger. The sales ledger is simply there to show the detail in the general ledger SLCA. The double entry for the £45 discount only takes place in the general ledger as we have seen between the SLCA and the discounts allowed account.

Activity 4

Your organisation receives a number of cheques from receivables through the post each day and these are listed on the cheque listing. It also makes some sales to non-credit customers each day which include VAT at the standard rate of 20% and are paid for by cheque.

Today's date is 28 April 20X1 and the cash receipts book is given below:

Cash receipts book							
Date	Narrative	SL Code	Discount £	Bank £	SLCA £	Sales £	VAT 20% £
20X1							
28/4	G Heilbron	SL04		108.45	108.45		
	L Tessa	SL15	3.31	110.57	110.57		
	J Dent	SL17	6.32	210.98	210.98		
	F Trainer	SL21		97.60	97.60		
	A Winter	SL09	3.16	105.60	105.60		
	Non-credit sales			270.72		225.60	45.12
			12.79	903.92	633.20	225.60	45.12

Required:

Show what the entries in the sales ledger will be:

Account name	Amount £	Dr ✓	Cr ✓

Show what the entries in the general ledger will be:

Account name	Amount £	Dr ✓	Cr ✓

4.4 Recording cash payments

The PDB is often used only for invoices from suppliers of purchases, i.e. goods for resale. Invoices for rent, electricity, telephone, etc will typically not be entered in the PDB. They will be paid by cheque, and the double entry will be made directly between the cash payments book and the relevant expense account in the general ledger.

One reason for this is that the purchases day book (like the sales day book) is used because the business will typically have a large number of similar transactions (e.g. purchases of goods for resale). To simplify the accounting these are all listed in the PDB and posted in total to the general ledger. Payment of rent or telephone only happens once every three months so there is no need to group these together; they are easily dealt with on an individual basis.

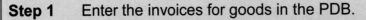

Example

Parma Products buys goods for resale from two suppliers on credit. The business buys £1,000 + VAT at 20% of goods from X and £3,000 + VAT at 20% of goods from Y. Parma receives an invoice and pays £500 + VAT at 20% rent to their landlord. Parma also pays X's invoice in full. Enter these transactions in the accounts of Parma Products. The rent invoice is not entered in the PDB.

Solution

Step 1 Enter the invoices for goods in the PDB.

PURCHASES DAY BOOK						
Date	Supplier	Reference	Invoice number	Total £	VAT £	Purchases £
	X			1,200	200	1,000
	Y			3,600	600	3,000
			TOTALS	4,800	800	4,000

Step 2 Enter the totals of the PDB in the general ledger.

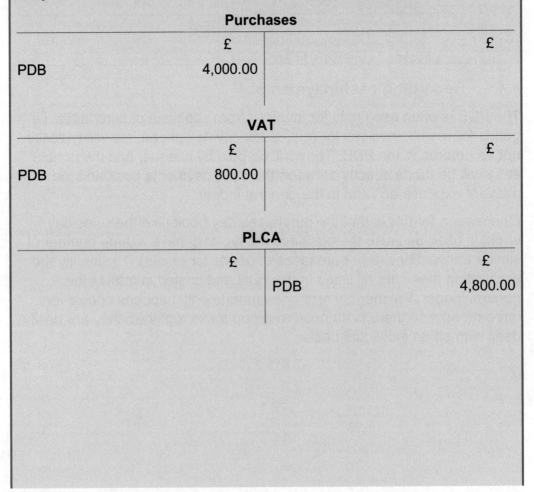

Purchases

	£		£
PDB	4,000.00		

VAT

	£		£
PDB	800.00		

PLCA

	£		£
		PDB	4,800.00

Step 3   Enter the cash paid in the analysed cash payments book.

Date	Narrative	Reference	Total	VAT	PLCA	Rent	Discount received
CASH PAYMENTS BOOK							
			£	£	£	£	£
	X		1,200.00		1,200.00		
	Rent		600.00	100.00		500.00	
		TOTALS	1,800.00	100.00	1,200.00	500.00	

Note that the VAT on the payment to the supplier has already been accounted for in the general ledger via the entries in the PDB. However, the rent invoice was not entered in the PDB and so the VAT has to be entered in the VAT column of the cash book from where it will be posted to the VAT account (see Step 4).

Step 4   Post the cash paid totals from the cash book to the general ledger.

Purchases

	£		£
PDB	4,000.00		

VAT

	£		£
PDB	800.00		
CPB	100.00		

PLCA

	£		£
CPB	1,200.00	PDB	4,800.00

Rent

	£		£
CPB	500.00		

Note 1: All the VAT paid is now debited to the VAT account. You must make sure that you understand how some is posted via the PDB and some via the cash book.

Note 2: All of the entries made from the cash payments book are debit entries. The credit entry is the total of the cash payments (£1,800) since the cash payments book is part of the double entry.

Step 5: Enter the amounts in the purchases ledger.

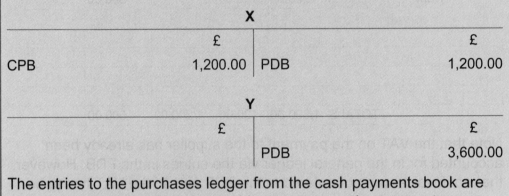

X

	£		£
CPB	1,200.00	PDB	1,200.00

Y

	£		£
		PDB	3,600.00

The entries to the purchases ledger from the cash payments book are debit entries in the individual payable accounts as the payment means that less is owed to the payable.

4.5 Settlement discounts received from suppliers

Settlement discounts are a tricky complication when dealing with the analysed purchases day book and cash book.

Example

Consider a business run by Francis which buys goods costing £2,000 + VAT from Z. Z offers a 5% settlement discount if Francis pays within 30 days. Francis pays within 30 days.

Enter these new transactions in the books of Francis.

Solution

Step 1 Calculate the value of the invoice.

	£
Cost of goods	2,000.00
VAT (2,000 – (5% × 2,000)) × 20%	380.00
Total invoice value	2,380.00

Step 2   Enter the invoice from Z in the purchases day book.

PURCHASES DAY BOOK

Date	Supplier	Reference	Invoice number	Total £	VAT £	Purchases £
	Z			2,380.00	380.00	2,000.00
			TOTALS	2,380.00	380.00	2,000.00

Step 3   Enter the totals of the purchases day book in the general ledger.

Purchases

	£		£
PDB	2,000.00		

VAT

	£		£
PDB	380.00		

PLCA

	£		£
		PDB	2,380.00

Step 4   Calculate the cash paid by Francis.

	£
Cost of goods	2,000.00
5% settlement discount	(100.00)
	1,900.00
VAT (2,000–(5% × 2,000)) × 20%	380.00
Total cash paid	2,280.00

Step 5   Enter the cash paid in the analysed cash payments book.

CASH PAYMENTS BOOK							
Date	Narrative	Reference	Total	VAT	PLCA	Rent	Discount received
			£	£	£	£	£
	Z		2,280.00		2,280.00		100.00
		TOTALS	2,280.00		2,280.00		100.00

Note: Remember that the discount received column is a 'memorandum' account. The cash book only cross-casts if you ignore the discount received column.

Step 6   Post the cash payments book totals to the general ledger.

Purchases

	£		£
PDB	2,000.00		

VAT

	£		£
PDB	380.00		

PLCA

	£		£
CPB	2,280.00	PDB	2,380.00
Discount received	100.00		

Discount received

	£		£
		PLCA	100.00

Activity 5

Given below is the cash payments book for a business.

							CASH PAYMENTS BOOK	
Date	Details	Cheque no	Code	Discount £	Bank £	PLCA £	Cash purchases £	VAT £
12/3	Homer Ltd	03648	PL12	5.06	168.70	168.70		
	Forker & Co	03649	PL07	5.38	179.45	179.45		
	Purchases	03650			342.00		285.00	57.00
	Print Ass.	03651	PL08		190.45	190.45		
	ABG Ltd	03652	PL02	6.62	220.67	220.67		
	Purchases	03653			198.00		165.00	33.00
	G Greg	03654	PL19		67.89	67.89		
				17.06	1,367.16	827.16	450.00	90.00

Required:

Show what the entries in the purchases ledger will be:

Account name	Amount £	Dr ✓	Cr ✓

Show what the entries in the general ledger will be:

Account name	Amount £	Dr ✓	Cr ✓

5 The cash book as part of the general ledger

The PBKT assessment may show the cashbook as a ledger account format. This means that the cashbook actually forms a part of the general ledger, with the entries being one side of the double entry required within the general ledger. Therefore a typical assessment requirement will be to complete the other side of the entry within the general ledger, and to update the individual accounts in the subsidiary ledger.

Example 1

Date	Detail	Disc Allow	Bank £	Date	Detail	Bank £
30/6/X9	Bal b/d		16,173	30/6/X9	Plant & machinery	25,500
30/6/X9	Receiv able A	342	13,200	30/6/X9	Loan repayment	1,500
				30/6/X9	Motor expenses	1,440
				30/6/X9	Bal c/d	933
		342	29,373			29,373

We need to appreciate that the bank account has already been completed with one side of the entries, and the other side of the entry is all that is required in order to complete the double entry postings.

It is also important to note that the discount column is still to be treated as a memorandum column, requiring both the debit and the credit entries.

Postings to general ledger (ignoring VAT)

Account	Amount	Dr or Cr
SLCA	13,200	Cr
Plant and machinery	25,500	Dr
Loan	1,500	Dr
Motor expenses	1,440	Dr
SLCA	342	Cr
Discount allowed	342	Dr

Postings to the sales ledger

Account	Amount	Dr or Cr
Receivable A account	13,200	Cr
Receivable A account	342	Cr

Activity 6

Date	Detail	Bank £	Date	Detail	VAT £	Bank £
30/6/X9	Bal b/d	24,067	30/6/X9	Motor vehicles		20,000
30/6/X9	Bal c/d	2,913	30/6/X9	Motor expenses	80	480
			30/6/X9	Payable B		6,500
		26,980			**80**	**26,980**
			1/7/X9	Bal b/d		2,913

What are the postings to the general and purchases ledgers?

Example 2

You may be asked to only record transactions for one side of the cash book.

Cashbook – debit side

Details	Discount £	Bank £
Balance b/f		2,568
Edwards Ltd	36	3,864

(a)   Record the TWO transactions within the sales ledger.

(b)   Record the THREE transactions within the general ledger.

Solution

It is important to appreciate that the above is still the cashbook as a ledger account, but only one half is required. Therefore, the entries will be the same as previously shown.

(a)   **Sales ledger**

Details	Amount £	Debit/Credit
Edwards Ltd	3,864	Credit
Edwards Ltd	36	Credit

(b)   **General ledger**

Details	Amount £	Debit/Credit
Sales ledger control account	3,864	Credit
Discounts allowed	36	Debit
Sales ledger control account	36	Credit

Activity 7

Cashbook – credit side

Details	VAT £	Bank £
Motor expenses	60	360
Wages		4,785

Record the THREE transactions within the general ledger.

Details	Amount £	Debit/Credit

6 Petty cash

Definition

Petty cash is the small amount of cash that most businesses hold in order to make small cash payments, such as payment for coffee and milk for the staff kitchen.

6.1 Petty cash box

Holding cash on business premises is a security risk and therefore it is important that the petty cash is secure. It should be kept in a locked petty cash box and usually this itself will be held in the safe. Only the person responsible for the petty cash should have access to the petty cash box.

6.2   Payment of petty cash

Petty cash is usually reimbursed to employees who have already incurred a small cash expense on behalf of the business. These payments should only be made for valid business expenses. For this reason, the petty cashier should only pay out to the employee on receipt of an authorised petty cash voucher and, where appropriate, VAT receipt.

> ### 🔍 Definition
>
> A petty cash voucher is an internal document that details the business expenditure that an employee has incurred out of his own money.

This voucher must be authorised by an appropriate person before any amounts can be paid to that employee out of the petty cash box.

A typical petty cash voucher is shown below:

	PETTY CASH VOUCHER			
Authorised by F R Clarke	**Received by** L Kent		No 4173	
Date	**Description**		**Amount**	
4 April 20X1	Train Fare		12	50
	Total		12	50

Signature of person authorising voucher

Signature of claimant

Sequential voucher number

Details of expenditure including the date and the nature of the expense

Total paid to employee

6.3   Maintaining petty cash records

Upon the petty cash vouchers being received and the employees being reimbursed, the details are recorded in the petty cash book. In Chapter 2 we were briefly introduced to the petty cash book as a book of prime entry. The PBKT assessment requires you to be able to make entries into the petty cash book.

6.4 Writing up the petty cash book

When cash is originally paid into the petty cash book then this will be recorded on the receipts side (debit side) of the petty cash book.

Each petty cash voucher will then in turn be written up in the petty cash book on the payments side.

To ensure that no vouchers have been mislaid, petty cash vouchers are pre-numbered sequentially. Each voucher is then entered into the petty cash book in the correct order, with each item of expenditure being recorded in the correct expense analysis column.

Example

A business has just started to run a petty cash system with an amount of £100. £100 is withdrawn from the bank account and paid into the petty cash box on 3 April 20X1.

During the first week the following authorised petty cash vouchers were paid. These transactions will now be recorded in the petty cash book.

PETTY CASH VOUCHER				
Authorised by T Smedley	Received by P Lannall	No	0001	
Date	Description		Amount	
3 April 20X1	Tea/coffee/milk		4	73
	Total		4	73

PETTY CASH VOUCHER				
Authorised by T Smedley	Received by R Sellers	No	0002	
Date	Description		Amount	
3 April 20X1	Train fare		14	90
	Total		14	90

PETTY CASH VOUCHER

Authorised by T Smedley	Received by F Dorne	No	0003	
Date	Description		Amount	
4 April 20X1	Stationery		4	00
	VAT		0	80
	Total		4	80

PETTY CASH VOUCHER

Authorised by T Smedley	Received by P Dent	No	0004	
Date	Description		Amount	
5 April 20X1	Postage costs		16	35
	Total		16	35

PETTY CASH VOUCHER

Authorised by T Smedley	Received by H Polly	No	0005	
Date	Description		Amount	
7 April 20X1	Train fare		15	30
	Total		15	30

PETTY CASH VOUCHER			
Authorised by T Smedley	Received by P Lannall	No	0006
Date	Description		Amount
8 April 20X1	Milk/biscuits		3 | 85
		Total	3 | 85

Solution

Petty cash book											
Receipts			Payments								
Date	Narrative	Total	Date	Narrative	Voucher no	Total	Postage	Travel	Tea & coffee	Sundry	VAT
20X1		£	20X1			£	£	£	£	£	£
03/04	Cash	100.00	03/04	Tea/coffee	0001	4.73			4.73		
			03/04	Train fare	0002	14.90		14.90			
			04/04	Stationery	0003	4.80				4.00	0.80
			05/04	Postage	0004	16.35	16.35				
			07/04	Train fare	0005	15.30		15.30			
			08/04	Milk/biscuits	0006	3.85			3.85		

6.5   The imprest system

Many businesses use the imprest system for petty cash. Using an imprest system makes petty cash easier to control and therefore reduces the possibility of error and fraud.

The business decides on a fixed amount of petty cash (the imprest) which is just large enough to cover normal petty cash requirements for a period (usually a week). This amount of petty cash is withdrawn from the bank.

Claims are paid out of petty cash by a voucher being completed for each amount of petty cash paid out. The vouchers are kept in the petty cash box so that the amount of cash held decreases and is replaced by vouchers.

At any given time, the total contents of the box (i.e. petty cash plus amounts withdrawn represented by vouchers) should equal the amount of the imprest.

At the end of the period, a cheque is drawn for the total of the vouchers which restores the petty cash float to the amount of the imprest. The vouchers are removed from the petty cash box and filed.

> ### ☀️ Example
>
> The imprest amount for a petty cash system is £150, which is the amount paid into the petty cash box on 1 November. At the end of the week the total of the vouchers in the petty cash box is £125.05. How much cash is required in order to replenish the petty cash box to the imprest amount?
>
> **Solution**
>
> £125.05, the amount paid out on the basis of the petty cash vouchers.

6.6 Non-imprest petty cash system

An imprest petty cash system as in the previous example is the most common method of dealing with and controlling petty cash. However some businesses may use a non-imprest system. This might be where a set amount of cash is withdrawn each week and paid into the petty cash box no matter what the level of expenditure in that week.

For example it may be an organisation's policy to cash a cheque for £50 each Monday morning for use as petty cash for the week. The danger here is either that petty cash requirements are more than £50 in the week in which case the petty cash box will run out of money. Alternatively week after week expenditure is significantly less than £50 each week, leading to a large amount of cash building up in the petty cash box.

6.7 Posting the petty cash book

Once the petty cash book has been written up, we must now post the totals of the petty cash book to the general ledger accounts.

The petty cash book can be a book of prime entry alone, or a book of prime entry that also forms part of the double entry bookkeeping system.

6.8 Posting the petty cash receipt

The receipt into the petty cash box has come from cash being withdrawn from the bank account. This will have been done by writing out a cheque for cash and withdrawing this from the bank. Therefore the cheque should be recorded in the cash payments book as a payment when the cash payments book is written up.

The receipt of the cash into the petty cash box is recorded in the receipts side of the petty cash book, debit side.

6.9 Posting the petty cash payments – the petty cash book as part of the double entry bookkeeping system

We will consider an example where the petty cash book is part of the double entry bookkeeping system as well as being a book of prime entry.

Example

A petty cash book is give below. This is to be posted to the general ledger accounts.

Petty cash book

Receipts			Payments								
Date	Narrative	Total	Date	Narrative	Voucher no	Total	Postage	Travel	Tea & coffee	Sundry	VAT
20X1		£	20X1			£	£	£	£	£	£
20/08	Bal b/d	100.00	20/08	Tea/coffee	0001	13.68			13.68		
20/08	Bank	50.00	21/08	Train fare	0002	6.80		6.80			
			21/08	Stationery	0003	19.20				16.00	3.20
			22/08	Postage	0004	16.35	16.35				
			23/08	Train fare	0005	15.30		15.30			
			24/08	Milk/biscuits	0006	3.85			3.85		

Solution

Step 1 Each of the columns in the petty cash payments side must be totalled.

The accuracy of your totalling should be checked by ensuring that all of the analysis column totals add back to the total of the 'total' column in the petty cash book payments side.

Petty cash book

Receipts			Payments								
Date	Narrative	Total	Date	Narrative	Voucher no	Total	Postage	Travel	Tea & coffee	Sundry	VAT
20X1		£	20X1			£	£	£	£	£	£
20/08	Bal b/d	100.00	20/08	Tea/coffee	0001	13.68			13.68		
20/08	Bank	50.00	21/08	Train fare	0002	6.80		6.80			
			21/08	Stationery	0003	19.20				16.00	3.20
			22/08	Postage	0004	16.35	16.35				
			23/08	Train fare	0005	15.30		15.30			
			24/08	Milk/biscuits	0006	3.85			3.85		
		150.00				75.18	16.35	22.10	17.53	16.00	3.20

Check the totals:

	£
Postage	16.35
Travel	22.10
Tea and coffee	17.53
Sundry	16.00
VAT	3.20
	75.18

Step 2 Each of the analysis column totals must now be entered into the general ledger accounts as debit entries.

VAT account

	£		£
Petty cash book (PCB)	3.20		

The entry has come from the petty cash book and this is the reference – this is now shortened to PCB.

Postage account

	£		£
PCB	16.35		

Travel account

	£		£
PCB	22.10		

Tea and coffee account

	£		£
PCB	17.53		

Sundry expenses account

	£		£
PCB	16.00		

Bank account

	£		£
		PCB	50.00

There is no need for an entry to the petty cash control account as the petty cash book acts as the general ledger account and the closing balance on the account is taken from it when the trial balance is prepared.

6.10 Posting the petty cash payments – the petty cash book not part of the double entry bookkeeping system

When the petty cash book is not part of the double entry system, the accounting entries must show the impact on the expense accounts, the VAT account and the petty cash control account.

In the event of there being a top up to the petty cash, a separate entry will be required. We would need to show the money being withdrawn from the bank and deposited into petty cash.

We will now consider the earlier illustration to review the general ledger postings required when the petty cash book is not part of the double entry accounting system.

Example

A petty cash book is give below. This is to be posted to the general ledger accounts.

Petty cash book											
Receipts			**Payments**								
Date	Narrative	Total	Date	Narrative	Voucher no	Total	Postage	Travel	Tea & coffee	Sundry	VAT
20X1		£	20X1			£	£	£	£	£	£
20/08	Bal b/d	100.00	20/08	Tea/coffee	0001	13.68			13.68		
20/08	Bank	50.00	21/08	Train fare	0002	6.80		6.80			
			21/08	Stationery	0003	19.20				16.00	3.20
			22/08	Postage	0004	16.35	16.35				
			23/08	Train fare	0005	15.30		15.30			
			24/08	Milk/biscuits	0006	3.85			3.85		

Solution

Step 1 Each of the columns in the petty cash payments side must be totalled.

The accuracy of your totalling should be checked by ensuring that all of the analysis column totals add back to the total of the 'total' column in the petty cash book payments side.

Petty cash book										
Receipts			Payments							
Date	Narrative	Total	Date	Narrative	Voucher no	Total	Postage	Travel	Tea & coffee	Sundry	VAT
20X1		£	20X1			£	£	£	£	£	£
20/08	Bal b/d	100.00	20/08	Tea/coffee	0001	13.68			13.68		
20/08	Bank	50.00	21/08	Train fare	0002	6.80		6.80			
			21/08	Stationery	0003	19.20				16.00	3.20
			22/08	Postage	0004	16.35	16.35				
			23/08	Train fare	0005	15.30		15.30			
			24/08	Milk/biscuits	0006	3.85			3.85		
		150.00				75.18	16.35	22.10	17.53	16.00	3.20

Check the totals:

	£
Postage	16.35
Travel	22.10
Tea and coffee	17.53
Sundry	16.00
VAT	3.20
	75.18

We have been told that the petty cash book is not part of the double entry accounting system. The expense accounts of postage, travel, tea and coffee, sundry along with the VAT account will be debited, the corresponding impact on the petty cash control account will be to credit it (to reduce the balance) by the amount in total that has been paid out.

Remember that the account name in the general ledger should always match the analysis column headings in the petty cash-book and not the description of the expense given in the 'Details' column.

We must also record the impact of the top-up to the petty cash from the bank account. This will be shown as a credit from the bank ledger account and a debit to the petty cash control account.

Step 2   We will now make the entries required into the general ledger accounts.

VAT account

	£		£
Petty cash book (PCB)	3.20		

The entry has come from the petty cash book and this is the reference – this is now shortened to PCB.

Postage account

	£		£
PCB	16.35		

Travel account

	£		£
PCB	22.10		

Tea and coffee account

	£		£
PCB	17.53		

Sundry expenses account

	£		£
PCB	16.00		

Bank account

	£		£
		PCB	50.00

Petty cash control

	£		£
Balance b/d	100.00	PCB	75.18
Bank	50.00		

Activity 8

Summary of petty cash vouchers in hand at 31 October 20X7

Date	Description	Total £	VAT included £
1/10	Envelopes (Administration)	19.72	3.28
4/10	Cleaner (Administration)	8.75	
6/10	Food for staff lunch (Marketing)	17.13	
6/10	Taxi fares (Marketing)	16.23	
6/10	Rail fares (Marketing)	43.75	
10/10	Postage (Administration)	4.60	
15/10	Tea and coffee (Production)	4.39	
17/10	Light bulbs and refuse sacks (Distribution)	8.47	1.41
20/10	Flowers for reception (Administration)	21.23	
26/10	Cleaner (Administration)	8.75	

(a)   Write up the payments side of the petty cash book for October 20X7 from the information given.

You should allocate a sequential voucher number to each entry in the petty cash book. The last voucher number to be allocated in September was 6578.

Use the blank petty cash book provided.

(b)   Total each of the columns in the petty cash book and cross-cast them.

(c)   Post the totals to the general ledger accounts given.

PETTY CASH BOOK – PAYMENTS													
Date	Voucher no	Total		Production		Distribu-tion		Marketing		Administration		VAT	
		£		£		£		£		£		£	

Production expenses account

£	£

Distribution expenses account

£	£

Marketing expenses account

£	£

Administration expenses account

£	£

VAT account

£	£

6.11 Reconciling the petty cash

We saw earlier in the chapter that when an imprest system is being used for petty cash then at any point in time the amount of cash in the petty cash box plus the total of the vouchers in the petty cash box should equal the imprest amount.

At regular intervals, usually at the end of each week, this check will be carried out.

6.12 Procedure for reconciling the petty cash box

The total amount of cash in the petty cash box will be counted. The vouchers that have been paid during the week are also in the petty cash box and they must also be totalled.

When the amount of cash is added to the total of the vouchers in the box they should equal the imprest amount.

The petty cash vouchers for the week will then be removed from the box and filed.

Example

The amount of cash remaining in a petty cash box at the end of a week is as follows:

Notes/coins	Quantity
£10	1
£5	2
£2	3
£1	7
50p	9
20p	10
10p	15
5p	7
2p	16
1p	23

The imprest amount is £100 and the vouchers in the petty cash box at the end of the week are as follows:

PETTY CASH VOUCHER				
Authorised by C Alexi	Received by P Trant		No	0467
Date	Description		Amount	
4 May 20X3	Window cleaner		15	00
		Total	15	00

PETTY CASH VOUCHER			
Authorised by C Alexi	*Received by* F Saint	*No* 0468	
Date	*Description*	*Amount*	
5 May 20X3	Train fare	9	80
	Total	9	80

PETTY CASH VOUCHER			
Authorised by C Alexi	*Received by* A Paul	*No* 0469	
Date	*Description*	*Amount*	
5 May 20X3	Stationery	8	00
	VAT	1	60
	Total	9	60

PETTY CASH VOUCHER			
Authorised by C Alexi	*Received by* P Peters	*No* 0470	
Date	*Description*	*Amount*	
7 May 20X3	Postage	6	80
	Total	6	80

PETTY CASH VOUCHER			
Authorised by C Alexi	*Received by* C Ralph	*No* 0471	
Date	*Description*	*Amount*	
5 May 20X3	Train fare	16	90
	Total	16	90

The cash and vouchers in the petty cash box at the end of the week are to be reconciled.

Solution

The petty cash must be totalled:

Notes/coins	Quantity	Amount £
£10	1	10.00
£5	2	10.00
£2	3	6.00
£1	7	7.00
50p	9	4.50
20p	10	2.00
10p	15	1.50
5p	7	0.35
2p	16	0.32
1p	23	0.23
		———
		41.90
		———

Now the vouchers must be totalled.

	£
0467	15.00
0468	9.80
0469	9.60
0470	6.80
0471	16.90
	———
	58.10
	———

Finally, total the cash and the vouchers to ensure that they add back to the imprest amount.

	£
Cash	41.90
Vouchers	58.10
	———
	100.00
	———

6.13 Possible causes of difference

If there is more cash in the petty cash box than the balance on the petty cash control account this could be due to an error in writing up the petty cash book as more has been recorded in payments than has actually been paid out. In this case the entries in the petty cash book should be checked to the underlying petty cash vouchers to discover the error.

If there is less cash in the petty cash box than the balance on the petty cash control account this could also be due to an error in writing up the petty cash book as this time less payments have been recorded in the petty cash control account than were actually made. This may be due to a petty cash voucher having been omitted from the petty cash book and therefore again the underlying petty cash vouchers should all be checked to their entries in the petty cash book.

If no accounting errors or posting errors can be found then the cause is likely to be one of the following:

- an error has been made in paying a petty cash voucher and more money was handed out than was recorded on the voucher
- cash has been paid out of the petty cash box without a supporting voucher
- cash could have been stolen from the petty cash box.

In such cases the matter should be investigated and security of the petty cash and petty cash procedures improved.

Activity 9

Your business runs a petty cash box based upon an imprest amount of £60. This morning you have emptied the petty cash box and found the following notes, coins and vouchers.

Notes
£5 × 2

Coins
£1 × 3
50p × 5
20p × 4
10p × 6
5p × 7
2p × 10
1p × 8

Vouchers	£
2143	10.56
2144	3.30
2145	9.80
2146	8.44
2147	2.62
2148	6.31
2149	1.44

You are required to reconcile the cash and the vouchers in the petty cash box.

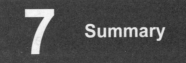

7 Summary

This chapter has reviewed over all aspects of making and receiving payments. The previous chapters have taken us through making credit sales and credit purchases, the documents and processes involved and how to record these transactions in the general and subsidiary ledgers.

In this chapter we have completed the sales and purchases cycle by reviewing the purpose and content of statements of accounts for receivables and from payables, what a remittance advice is and how to enter transactions into the cash book and make entries from the cash book to the general and subsidiary ledgers. Finally, the chapter reviews the maintenance of a petty cash system.

Answers to chapter activities

Activity 1

Thames Traders

To: Jack Johnson

Date: 31 May 20X6:

STATEMENT

Date	Transaction	Debit £	Credit £	Balance £
03 May	Inv 1848	38.79		38.79
07 May	Inv 1863	50.70		89.49
08 May	CN 446		12.40	77.09
10 May	Inv 1870	80.52		157.61
15 May	Payment		77.09	80.52
18 May	Inv 1881	42.40		122.92
23 May	Inv 1892	61.20		184.12
24 May	CN 458		16.50	167.62
30 May	Inv 1904	27.65		195.27

May we remind you that our credit terms are 30 days

Activity 2

False. A remittance advice is a slip that the customer can send back to the supplier with his payment to identify what the payment is for.

Activity 3

(a)   No

(b)   Any two from the following:

   (i)   The cheque has not been signed.

   (ii)   The cheque is out of date.

   (iii)   The words and figures on the cheque are not the same.

Activity 4

The entries in the sales ledger will be:

Account name	Amount £	Dr ✓	Cr ✓
G Heilbron	108.45		✓
L Tessa	110.57		✓
L Tessa	3.31		✓
J Dent	210.98		✓
J Dent	6.32		✓
F Trainer	97.60		✓
A Winter	105.60		✓
A Winter	3.16		✓

The entries in the general ledger will be:

Account name	Amount £	Dr ✓	Cr ✓
Discounts allowed	12.79	✓	
Sales ledger control account	12.79		✓
Sales ledger control account	633.20		✓
Sales	225.60		✓
VAT	45.12		✓

Activity 5

The entries in the purchases ledger will be:

Account name	Amount £	Dr ✓	Cr ✓
Homer Ltd	168.70	✓	
Homer Ltd	5.06	✓	
Forker & Co	179.45	✓	
Forker & Co	5.38	✓	
Print Ass.	190.45	✓	
ABG Ltd	220.67	✓	
ABG Ltd	6.62	✓	
G Greg	67.89	✓	

The entries in the general ledger will be:

Account name	Amount £	Dr ✓	Cr ✓
Discounts received	17.06		✓
Purchases ledger control account	17.06	✓	
Purchases ledger control account	827.16	✓	
Purchases	450.00	✓	
VAT	90.00	✓	

Activity 6

Postings to general ledger

Account	Amount	Dr or Cr
Motor vehicle	20,000	Dr
Motor expenses	400	Dr
VAT	80	Dr
PLCA	6,500	Dr

Postings to the purchases ledger

Account	Amount	Dr or Cr
Payable B account	6,500	Dr

Activity 7

Details	Amount £	Debit/Credit
Motor expenses	300	Debit
VAT	60	Debit
Wages	4,785	Debit

Activity 8

(a), (b)

		PETTY CASH BOOK – PAYMENTS											
Date	Voucher no	Total £		Production £		Distribution £		Marketing £		Administration £		VAT £	
01/10/X7	6579	19	72							16	44	3	28
04/10/X7	6580	8	75							8	75		
06/10/X7	6581	17	13					17	13				
06/10/X7	6582	16	23					16	23				
06/10/X7	6583	43	75					43	75				
10/10/X7	6584	4	60							4	60		
15/10/X7	6585	4	39	4	39								
17/10/X7	6586	8	47			7	06					1	41
20/10/X7	6587	21	23							21	23		
26/10/X7	6588	8	75							8	75		
		153	02	4	39	7	06	77	11	59	77	4	69

(c)

Production expenses account

	£		£
PCB	4.39		

Distribution expenses account

	£		£
PCB	7.06		

Marketing expenses account

	£		£
PCB	77.11		

Administration expenses account

	£		£
PCB	59.77		

VAT account

	£		£
PCB	4.69		

Activity 9

Notes and coins

	£	£
£5 × 2	10.00	
£1 × 3	3.00	
50p × 5	2.50	
20p × 4	0.80	
10p × 6	0.60	
5p × 7	0.35	
2p × 10	0.20	
1p × 8	0.08	
		17.53

Vouchers

	£	£
2143	10.56	
2144	3.30	
2145	9.80	
2146	8.44	
2147	2.62	
2148	6.31	
2149	1.44	
		42.47
Imprest amount		60.00

8 Test your knowledge

Workbook Activity 10

You work in the accounts department of Farmhouse Pickles Ltd and given below are two receivables' accounts from the sales ledger.

	Grant & Co				SL07
		£			£
1 April	Balance b/d	337.69	12 April	SRDB – 0335	38.70
4 April	SDB 32656	150.58	20 April	CRB	330.94
18 April	SDB 32671	179.52	20 April	CRB – discount	6.75
25 April	SDB 32689	94.36	24 April	SRDB – 0346	17.65

	Mitchell Partners				SL10
		£			£
1 April	Balance b/d	180.46	12 April	SRDB – 0344	66.89
7 April	SDB 32662	441.57	21 April	CRB	613.58
20 April	SDB 32669	274.57	21 April	CRB – discount	8.45

Required:

Prepare statements to be sent to each of these customers at the end of April 20X1 on the blank statements provided.

FARMHOUSE PICKLES LTD

225 School Lane
Weymouth
Dorset
WE36 5NR
Tel: 0261 480444
Fax: 0261 480555
Date:

To:

STATEMENT

Date	Transaction	Debit £	Credit £	Balance £

May we remind you that our credit terms are 30 days

<table>
<tr><td></td><td colspan="2">FARMHOUSE PICKLES LTD</td></tr>
</table>

To:

225 School Lane
Weymouth
Dorset
WE36 5NR
Tel: 0261 480444
Fax: 0261 480555
Date:

STATEMENT

Date	Transaction	Debit £	Credit £	Balance £

May we remind you that our credit terms are 30 days

Workbook Activity 11

Shown below is a customer's account from the sales ledger of Ryan's Toy Shop Ltd, along with a statement of account to be sent to that customer.

	Arnold's Toys Ltd						
Dr				Cr			
Date	Transaction	£		Date	Transaction	£	
19/11	Invoice 2195	118	08	20/11	Credit note 2198	323	60
20/11	Invoice 2198	2,201	95	22/11	Cheque	118	08
				22/11	Balance c/d	1,878	35
		2,320	03			2,320	03
23/11	Balance b/d	1,878	35				

Required:

Complete the statement of account below.

Ryan's Toy Shop LTD				
125 Finchley Way Bristol BS1 4PL Tel: 01272 200299				
STATEMENT OF ACCOUNT				
Customer name: Arnold's Toys Ltd				
Customer address: 14 High Street, Bristol, BS2 5FL				
Statement date 1st December		Amount		Balance
Date	Transaction	£	p	£	P

Workbook Activity 12

Simon Harris is a self-employed accountant who has a number of clients who all pay by cheque. Today's date is 5 May 20X1 and in the last week he has received the following cheques.

Required:

Inspect each one carefully to ensure that it is valid and make a note of any problems that you find.

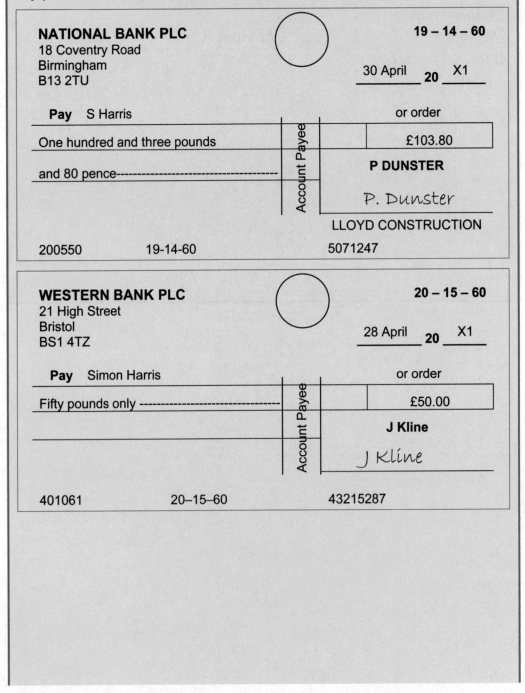

NATIONAL BANK PLC
18 Coventry Road
Birmingham
B13 2TU

19 – 14 – 60

30 April 20 X1

Pay S Harris   or order

One hundred and three pounds   £103.80

and 80 pence--   **P DUNSTER**

                                                                              P. Dunster

                                                                    LLOYD CONSTRUCTION

200550   19-14-60   5071247

WESTERN BANK PLC
21 High Street
Bristol
BS1 4TZ

20 – 15 – 60

28 April 20 X1

Pay Simon Harris   or order

Fifty pounds only --------------------------------   £50.00

                                                                              J Kline

                                                                              J Kline

401061   20–15–60   43215287

NORTHERN BANK PLC
68 Main Road
Warwick
B15 2KP

21– 18– 40

15 April **20** X1

Pay S Harris   or order

Forty eight pounds   £48.20

and 20 pence-----------------------------------   **K T LOPEZ**

Account Payee

461002   21–18–40   39761114

CENTRAL BANK PLC
44 Warwick Road
Birmingham
B6 4LK

16 – 20 – 30

1 May **20** X1

Pay S Harris   or order

One hundred and eighteen pounds   £118.50

and 50 pence-----------------------------------   **A RANKIN**

A Rankin

Account Payee

610400   16–20–30   32146921

NATIONAL BANK PLC
18 Coventry Road
Birmingham
B13 2TU

19 – 14 – 60

12 May **20** X1

Pay S Harris   or order

Two hundred and one pounds   £201.67

and 67 pence-----------------------------------   **L GARRY**

L Garry

Account Payee

201660   19-14-60   43012004

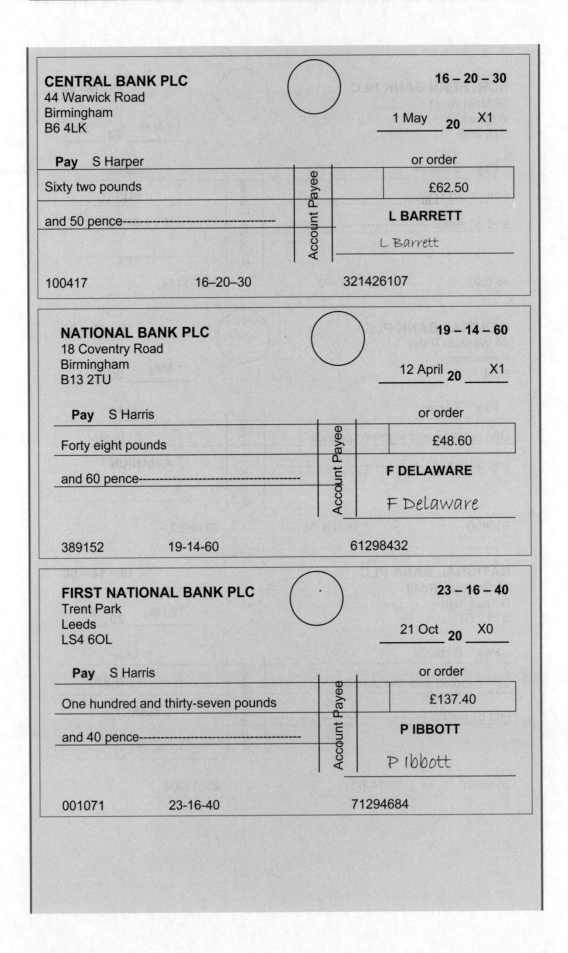

CENTRAL BANK PLC
44 Warwick Road
Birmingham
B6 4LK

16 – 20 – 30

1 May 20 X1

Pay S Harper   or order

Sixty two pounds   £62.50

and 50 pence--

Account Payee

L BARRETT

L Barrett

100417   16–20–30   321426107

NATIONAL BANK PLC
18 Coventry Road
Birmingham
B13 2TU

19 – 14 – 60

12 April 20 X1

Pay S Harris   or order

Forty eight pounds   £48.60

and 60 pence--

Account Payee

F DELAWARE

F Delaware

389152   19-14-60   61298432

FIRST NATIONAL BANK PLC
Trent Park
Leeds
LS4 6OL

23 – 16 – 40

21 Oct 20 X0

Pay S Harris   or order

One hundred and thirty-seven pounds   £137.40

and 40 pence---

Account Payee

P IBBOTT

P Ibbott

001071   23-16-40   71294684

NATIONAL BANK PLC
18 Coventry Road
Birmingham
B13 2TU

19 – 14 – 60

28 April **20** X1

Pay S Harris

or order

One hundred and thirty five pounds

Account Payee

£153.80

and 80 pence-------------------------------------

J LOVELL

J Lovell

041261   19-14-60   32114687

CENTRAL BANK PLC
44 Warwick Road
Birmingham
B6 4LK

16 – 20 – 30

1 May **20** X1

Pay S Harris

or order

Eighty pounds

Account Payee

£80.60

and 60 pence------------------------------------

G L ELLIS

G L eLLIS

104010   16–20–30   40162174

Workbook Activity 13

You work for Keyboard Supplies. Today's date is 12 May 20X1 and the following five cheques have arrived in this morning's post. You have found the invoices that these payments relate to – these are also given.

Required:

Check that each receipt is correct and make a note of any problems that you find.

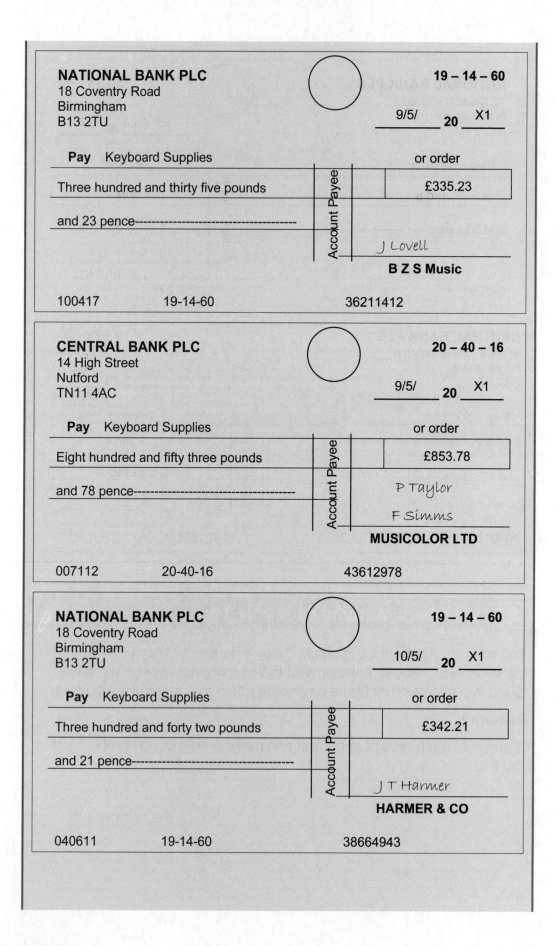

NATIONAL BANK PLC
18 Coventry Road
Birmingham
B13 2TU

19 – 14 – 60

9/5/ 20 X1

Pay Keyboard Supplies

or order

Three hundred and thirty five pounds

£335.23

and 23 pence--------------------------------------

Account Payee

J Lovell

B Z S Music

100417   19-14-60   36211412

CENTRAL BANK PLC
14 High Street
Nutford
TN11 4AC

20 – 40 – 16

9/5/ 20 X1

Pay Keyboard Supplies

or order

Eight hundred and fifty three pounds

£853.78

and 78 pence--------------------------------------

Account Payee

P Taylor

F Simms

MUSICOLOR LTD

007112   20-40-16   43612978

NATIONAL BANK PLC
18 Coventry Road
Birmingham
B13 2TU

19 – 14 – 60

10/5/ 20 X1

Pay Keyboard Supplies

or order

Three hundred and forty two pounds

£342.21

and 21 pence--------------------------------------

Account Payee

J T Harmer

HARMER & CO

040611   19-14-60   38664943

WESTERN BANK PLC
18 Coventry Road
Birmingham
B13 2TU

15 – 20 – 40

9/5/ 20 x1

Pay   Keyboard Supplies   or order

Nine hundred and twenty-one pounds   £921.88

and 88 pence-------------------------------------

Account Payee

SJ Newford
NEWFORD MUSIC

004128   15-20-40   82823937

FIRST NATIONAL BANK PLC
Main Square
Nottingham
NT2 4XY

20 – 14 – 60

10/5/ 20 X1

Pay   Keyboard Supplies   or order

Four hundred and thirty eight pounds   £438.06

and 6 pence-------------------------------------

Account Payee

T Gilchrist
Trent Music

201067   20-14-60   67112604

INVOICE

Invoice to:
BZS Music
42 Westhill
Nutford TN11 3PQ

Keyboard Supplies
Trench Park Estate
Fieldham
Sussex TN21 4AF
Tel: 01829 654545
Fax: 01829 654646

Deliver to:

Invoice no:	06180
Tax point:	3 May 20X1
VAT reg :	466 1128 30
Your reference:	SL01
Purchase order no:	77147

Code	Description	Quantity	VAT rate %	Unit price £	Amount excl of VAT £
B4012	Bento Keyboard	2	20	180.00	360.00
					360.00
Trade discount 20%					72.00
					288.00
VAT					55.87
Total amount payable					343.87

Deduct discount of 3% if paid within 10 days, net 30 days

INVOICE

Invoice to:
Musicolor Ltd
23 High Street
Nutford TN11 4 TZ

Keyboard Supplies
Trench Park Estate
Fieldham
Sussex TN21 4AF
Tel: 01829 654545
Fax: 01829 654646

Deliver to:

As above

Invoice no:	06176
Tax point:	1 May 20X1
VAT reg :	466 1128 30
Your reference:	SL06
Purchase order no:	6362

Code	Description	Quantity	VAT rate %	Unit price £	Amount excl of VAT £
Z4600	Zanni Keyboard	3	20	185.00	555.00
A4802	Atol Keyboard	2	20	130.00	260.00
					815.00
Trade discount 10%					81.50
					733.50
VAT					142.29
Total amount payable					875.79

Deduct discount of 3% if paid within 5 days, net 30 days

INVOICE

Invoice to:
Harmer & Co
1 Acre Street
Nutford TN11 0HA

Deliver to:

As above

Keyboard Supplies
Trench Park Estate
Fieldham
Sussex TN21 4AF
Tel: 01829 654545
Fax: 01829 654646

Invoice no:	06183
Tax point:	3 May 20X1
VAT reg no:	466 1128 30
Your reference:	SL17
Purchase order no:	047786

Code	Description	Quantity	VAT rate %	Unit price £	Amount excl of VAT £
G4326	Garland Keyboard	3	20	98.00	294.00
					294.00

VAT	57.03
Total amount payable	351.03

Deduct discount of 3% if paid within 10 days, net 30 days

INVOICE

Invoice to:
Newford Music
32/34 Main Street
Welland
Sussex TN4 6BD

Keyboard Supplies
Trench Park Estate
Fieldham
Sussex TN21 4AF
Tel: 01829 654545
Fax: 01829 654646

Deliver to:

As above

Invoice no:	06171
Tax point:	30 April 20X1
VAT reg :	466 1128 30
Your reference:	SL18
Purchase order no:	47202

Code	Description	Quantity	VAT rate %	Unit price £	Amount excl of VAT £
Z4406	Zanni Keyboard	6	20	165.00	990.00
					990.00
Trade discount 20%					198.00
					792.00
VAT					153.64
Total amount payable					945.64

Deduct discount of 3% if paid within 10 days, net 30 days

INVOICE

Keyboard Supplies

Invoice to:
Trent Music
Trent House
Main Street
Fieldham TN21 6ZF

Trench Park Estate
Fieldham
Sussex TN21 4AF
Tel: 01829 654545
Fax: 01829 654646

Deliver to:

Invoice no:	06184
Tax point:	3 May 20X1
VAT reg :	466 1128 30
Your reference:	SL41
Purchase order no:	93754

Code	Description	Quantity	VAT rate %	Unit price £	Amount excl of VAT £
G4030	Garland Keyboard	4	20	105.00	420.00
					420.00
Trade discount 10%					42.00
					378.00
VAT					73.33
Total amount payable					451.33

Deduct discount of 3% if paid within 10 days, net 30 days

Workbook Activity 14

Ellis Electricals makes the following credit sales to A and B giving a 20% trade discount plus a 5% settlement discount if customers pay their invoices within 30 days.

	Customer A £	Customer B £
Sales value	1,000	4,000
Trade discount (20%)	200	800
Net sales value	800	3,200
VAT (calculated on the net sales value after allowing for the settlement discount)		
Customer A: (800 − (800 × 5%)) × 20%	152	
Customer B: (3,200 − (3,200 × 5%)) × 20%		608
Total invoice value	952	3,808

Ellis Electricals also makes a cash sale to C for £300 plus VAT at 20%.

Remember that the VAT is calculated as if the settlement discount is taken whether the customer pays within 30 days and takes it or not – there is no going back to recalculate the VAT.

Customer A pays his invoice in full within 30 days and takes the settlement discount. Customer B pays £2,000 on account.

Task

Write up the SDB and the CRB and post the entries to the general and sales ledgers.

Workbook Activity 15

Given below is the debit side of the cash book completed for transactions that took place on 15 May:

Cash Book – Debit side				
Date	Narrative	SL Code	Discount £	Bank £
20X1				
15/5	McCaul & Partners	M04	2.95	147.56
	P Martin	M02		264.08
	F Little	L03		167.45
	D Raine	R01	7.97	265.89
			10.92	844.98

Required:

Show what the entries in the sales ledger will be:

Account name	Amount £	Dr ✓	Cr ✓

Show what the entries in the general ledger will be:

Account name	Amount £	Dr ✓	Cr ✓

Workbook Activity 16

Given below are four invoices received by Nethan Builders that are to be paid today, 18 May 20X1. It is the business policy to take advantage of any settlement discounts possible.

You are required to complete a remittance advice for each payment. The last cheque used was number 200549.

INVOICE

Invoice to:
Nethan Builders
Brecon House
Stamford Road
Manchester
M16 4PL

Deliver to:
As above

Building Contract Supplies
Unit 15
Royal Estate
Manchester
M13 2EF
Tel: 0161 562 3041
Fax: 0161 562 3042

Invoice no:	07742	
Tax point:	8 May 20X1	
VAT reg no:	776 4983 06	

Code	Description	Quantity	VAT rate %	Unit price £	Amount excl of VAT £
SDGSL6	SDGS Softwood 47 × 225 mm	20.5 m	20	8.30	170.15
					170.15
VAT					33.51
Total amount payable					203.66

Deduct discount of 1½% if paid within 14 days

INVOICE

Jenson Ltd

Invoice to:
Nethan Builders
Brecon House
Stamford Road
Manchester
M16 4PL

Deliver to:
As above

30 Longfield Park, Kingsway
M45 2TP
Tel: 0161 511 4666
Fax: 0161 511 4777

Invoice no:	47811
Tax point:	5 May 20X1
VAT reg no:	641 3229 45
Purchase order no:	7174

Code	Description	Quantity	VAT rate %	Unit price £	Amount excl of VAT £
PL432115	Door Lining set 32 × 115 mm	6	20	30.25	181.50
					181.50
Trade discount 15%					27.22
					154.28
VAT					29.93
Total amount payable					184.21

Deduct discount of 3% if paid within 10 days

INVOICE

Magnum Supplies

Invoice to:
Nethan Builders
Brecon House
Stamford Road
Manchester
M16 4PL

Deliver to:
As above

140/150 Park Estate
Manchester
M20 6EG
Tel: 0161 561 3202
Fax: 0161 561 3200

Invoice no:	077422
Tax point:	11 May 20X1
VAT reg no:	611 4337 90

Code	Description	Quantity	VAT rate %	Unit price £	Amount excl of VAT £
BH47732	House Bricks – Red	600	20	1.24	744.00
					744.00
Trade discount 15%					111.60
					632.40
VAT					123.95
Total amount payable					756.35

Deduct discount of 2% if paid within 10 days

INVOICE

Haddow Bros
The White House
Standing Way
Manchester
M13 6FH
Tel: 0161 560 3140
Fax: 0161 560 6140

Invoice to:
Nethan Builders
Brecon House
Stamford Road
Manchester
M16 4PL

Deliver to:
As above

Invoice no:	G33940
Tax point:	9 May 20X1
VAT reg no:	460 3559 71

Code	Description	Quantity	VAT rate %	Unit price £	Amount excl of VAT £
PLY8FE1	Plywood Hardwood 2440 × 1220 mm	24	20	17.80	427.20
					427.20
VAT					83.73
Total amount payable					510.93

Deduct discount of 2% if paid within 10 days

REMITTANCE ADVICE

To:

Nethan Builders
Brecon House
Stamford House
Manchester
M16 4PL

Tel: 0161 521 6411
Fax: 0161 530 6412
VAT reg: 471 3860 42
Date:

Date	Invoice no	Amount £	Discount taken £	Paid £

Total paid   £

Cheque no

REMITTANCE ADVICE

To:

Nethan Builders
Brecon House
Stamford House
Manchester
M16 4PL

Tel: 0161 521 6411
Fax: 0161 530 6412
VAT reg: 471 3860 42
Date:

Date	Invoice no	Amount £	Discount taken £	Paid £

Total paid   £

Cheque no

REMITTANCE ADVICE

To:

Nethan Builders
Brecon House
Stamford House
Manchester
M16 4PL

Tel: 0161 521 6411
Fax: 0161 530 6412
VAT reg: 471 3860 42
Date:

Date	Invoice no	Amount £	Discount taken £	Paid £

Total paid   £

Cheque no

REMITTANCE ADVICE

To:

Nethan Builders
Brecon House
Stamford House
Manchester
M16 4PL

Tel: 0161 521 6411
Fax: 0161 530 6412
VAT reg: 471 3860 42
Date:

Date	Invoice no	Amount £	Discount taken £	Paid £

Total paid   £

Cheque no _____

Workbook Activity 17

Given below is a business' petty cash book for the week.

Petty cash book

	Receipts				Payments					
Date	Narrative	Total	Date	Details	Voucher no	Amount £	Postage £	Staff welfare £	Station-ery £	Travel expenses £	VAT £
5/1/X1	Bal b/d	150.00	12/1/X1	Postage	03526	13.68	13.68				
				Staff welfare	03527	25.00		25.00			
				Stationery	03528	15.12			12.60		2.52
				Taxi fare	03529	12.25				10.21	2.04
				Staff welfare	03530	6.40		6.40			
				Postage	03531	12.57	12.57				
				Rail fare	03532	6.80				6.80	
				Stationery	03533	8.16			6.80		1.36
				Taxi fare	03534	19.20				16.00	3.20
						119.18	26.25	31.40	19.40	33.01	9.12

Required:

NB: The petty cash book also forms part of the general ledger. Show what the entries in the general ledger will be:

Account name	Amount £	Dr ✓	Cr ✓

Workbook Activity 18

Given below is a completed petty cash book for transactions that took place on 12 April 20X1:

Petty cash book

Receipts			Payments								
Date	Narrative	Total	Date	Narrative	Voucher no	Total	Postage	Staff welfare	Stationery	Travel expenses	VAT
						£	£	£	£	£	£
12/04	Bal b/d	100.00	12/04	Coffee/milk	2534	4.68		4.68			
				Postage	2535	13.26	13.26				
				Stationery	2536	10.48			8.74		1.74
				Taxi fare	2537	15.32				12.77	2.55
				Postage	2538	6.75	6.75				
				Train fare	2539	7.40				7.40	
				Stationery	2540	3.94			3.29		0.65
						61.83	20.01	4.68	12.03	20.17	4.94

Required:

Post the required entries to the general ledger accounts:

Postage

	£		£
Balance b/f	231.67		

Staff welfare

	£		£
Balance b/f	334.78		

Stationery

	£		£
Balance b/f	53.36		

Travel expenses

	£		£
Balance b/f	579.03		

VAT account

	£		£
		Balance b/f	967.44

Workbook Activity 19

A business runs its petty cash on an imprest system with an imprest amount of £100 per week.

At the end of the week ending 22 May 20X1 the vouchers in the petty cash box were:

Voucher no	£
02634	13.73
02635	8.91
02636	10.57
02637	3.21
02638	11.30
02639	14.66

The cash remaining in the petty cash box was made up as follows:

£10 note	1
£5 note	2
£2 coin	3
£1 coin	7
50p coin	5
20p coin	4
10p coin	1
5p coin	2
2p coin	3
1p coin	6

You are required to reconcile the petty cash in the box to the vouchers in the box at 22 May 20X1 and if it does not reconcile to suggest reasons for the difference.

WORKBOOK ACTIVITIES
ANSWERS

Workbook Activities Answers

1 Business documents

Workbook Activity 3

(a) To allow for expansion of the number of accounts in the general (main) ledger

(b) Any three from:

- Customer account codes
- Supplier account codes
- Product codes
- Inventory codes
- VAT codes
- Department codes

(c)

	TRUE/ FALSE
General ledger codes help when barcoding an item of inventory	FALSE
General ledger codes help when filing a financial document	FALSE
General ledger codes help trace relevant accounts quickly and easily	TRUE
General ledger codes help find the total amount owing to a supplier	FALSE

Workbook Activity 4

Invoice from:	Supplier account code	General ledger code
Haddow Bros	HAD29	GL112
Jenson Ltd	JEN32	GL140
AJ Broom & Company Ltd	AJB14	GL110
JM Bond & Co	JMB33	GL110

2 Books of prime entry

Workbook Activity 1

Sales day book						
Date	Invoice no	Customer name	Code	Total £	VAT £	Net £
20X1						
1/5	03466	Fraser & Co	SL14	154.41	25.73	128.68
	03467	Letterhead Ltd	SL03	309.48	51.58	257.90
2/5	03468	Jeliteen Traders	SL15	115.89	19.31	96.58
	CN0746	Garner & Co	SL12	(82.44)	(13.74)	(68.70)
3/5	03469	Harper Bros	SL22	321.78	53.63	268.15
	03470	Juniper Ltd	SL17	126.45	21.07	105.38
4/5	03471	H G Frank	SL30	353.60	58.93	294.67
	CN0747	Hill Traders	SL26	(141.21)	(23.53)	(117.68)
5/5	03472	Keller Assocs	SL07	132.69	22.11	110.58
				1,290.65	215.09	1,075.56

Workbook Activity 2

Date	Supplier	Total	VAT £	Zone 1 £	Zone 2 £	Zone 3 £
20X2						
14/9	Bradley Ltd	252.00	42.00	210.00		
	Hannah Ltd	564.24	94.04			470.20
	Spearritt Ltd	482.40	80.40	402.00		
	Lee Ltd	1,291.20	215.20		1,076.00	
	O'Meara Ltd	381.12	63.52			317.60
	Cattermole Ltd	74.92	12.48		62.44	
	Barrett Ltd	129.36	21.56	107.80		
		3,175.24	529.20	719.80	1,138.44	787.80

3 Double entry bookkeeping – introduction

Workbook Activity 1

(a) (i) Asset

(ii) Liability

(iii) Asset

(iv) Asset

(v) Asset

(vi) Asset

(b) Any 3 from the choice of:

- Shareholders (investors)
- Potential investors
- HMRC
- Banks
- Customers
- Suppliers
- Employees (of the business)
- Government

(c) 1   Dual effect – each transaction has two financial effects

2   Separate entity – the owner of the business and the business are seen as two separate entities. All transactions are recorded in the point of view of the business.

3   Accounting equation –
     Assets – Liabilities = Capital + Profit – Drawings

Workbook Activity 2

Answer 1

	Assets £		Capital £
Cash	10,000	Capital introduced	10,000

Answer 2

Dual effect

Increase inv.	£2,500	(↑ asset)	
Decrease cash	£2,500	(↓ asset)	

	Assets £		Capital £
Inventory	2,500	Capital introduced	10,000
Cash	7,500		
	10,000		10,000

Answer 3

Dual effect

Increase inv.	£2,000	(↑ asset)
Increase payable	£2,000	(↑ liability)

	Net assets £		Capital £
Inventory	4,500	Capital introduced	10,000
Cash	7,500		
	12,000		
Less: Payables	(2,000)		
	10,000		10,000

Answer 4

Dual effect

Increase NCA	£1,000	(↑ asset)
Decrease cash	£1,000	(↓ asset)

	Net assets £		Capital £
Non-current asset	1,000	Capital introduced	10,000
Inventory	4,500		
Cash	6,500		
	12,000		
Less: Payables	(2,000)		
	10,000		10,000

Answer 5

Dual effect

Increase cash	£3,000	(↑ asset)
Decrease inv.	£2,000	(↓ asset)
Increase profit	£1,000	(↑ profit)

	Net assets £			Capital £
Non-current asset	1,000		Capital introduced	10,000
Inventory	2,500		Profit	1,000
Cash	9,500			
	———			
	13,000			
Less: Payables	(2,000)			
	———			———
	11,000			11,000
	———			———

Answer 6

Dual effect

Inc. receivables	£5,000	(↑ asset)
Dec. inventory	£2,000	(↓. asset)
Increase profit	£3,000	(↑ profit)

	Net assets £			Capital £
Non-current asset	1,000		Capital introduced	10,000
Inventory	500		Profit	4,000
Receivables	5,000			
Cash	9,500			
	———			
	16,000			
Less: Payables	(2,000)			
	———			———
	14,000			14,000
	———			———

Answer 7

Dual effect

Decrease cash	£500	(↓ asset)
Decrease profit	£500	(↓ profit)

	Net assets £			Capital £
Non-current asset	1,000		Capital introduced	10,000
Inventory	500		Profit	3,500
Receivables	5,000			
Cash	9,000			
	15,500			
Less: Payables	(2,000)			
	13,500			13,500

Answer 8

Dual effect

Increase cash	£2,000	(↑ asset)
Increase loan	£2,000	(↑ liability)

	Net assets £			Capital £
Non-current asset	1,000		Capital introduced	10,000
Inventory	500		Profit	3,500
Receivables	5,000			
Cash	11,000			
	17,500			
Less: Payables	(2,000)			
Loan	(2,000)			
	13,500			13,500

The loan will be shown separately from payables for purchases, which are known as trade payables.

Answer 9

Dual effect

Decrease cash	£1,500	(↓ asset)
Decrease payables	£1,500	(↓ liability)

Net assets	£		Capital	£
Non-current asset	1,000		Capital introduced	10,000
Inventory	500		Profit	3,500
Receivables	5,000			
Cash	9,500			
	16,000			
Less: Payables	(500)			
Loan	(2,000)			
	13,500			13,500

Answer 10

Dual effect

Dec. receivables	£3,000	(↓ asset)
Increase cash	£3,000	(↑ asset)

Net assets	£		Capital	£
Non-current asset	1,000		Capital introduced	10,000
Inventory	500		Profit	3,500
Receivables	2,000			
Cash	12,500			
	16,000			
Less: Payables	(500)			
Loan	(2,000)			
	13,500			13,500

Answer 11

Dual effect

Decrease cash	£750	(↓ asset)
Increase drawings	£750	(↓ capital)

Net assets	£		Capital	£
Non-current asset	1,000	Capital		10,000
Inventory	500	Profit		3,500
Receivables	2,000			
Cash	11,750			
	15,250			13,500
Less: Payables	(500)	Less: Drawings		(750)
Loan	(2,000)			
	12,750			12,750

We do not simply deduct drawings from profit as we want to show separately the profit or loss for the period before any drawings were made.

Workbook Activity 3

(a) Opening capital

	£		£
Assets Cash	5,000	Capital	5,000

(b) Cash purchase

	£		£
Assets Inventory	500	Capital	5,000
Cash (5,000 – 500)	4,500		
	5,000		5,000

(c) Credit purchase

	£		£
Assets Inventory (500+(5×200))	1,500	Capital	5,000
Cash	4,500		
	6,000		
Liabilities Payables	(1,000)		
	5,000		5,000

(d) **Cash sale**

	£		£
Assets Inventory (1,500 – 500)	1,000	Capital	5,000
Cash (4,500 + 750)	5,250	Profit (750 – 500)	250
	6,250		
Liabilities Payables	(1,000)		
	5,250		5,250

(e) **Cash sale**

	£		£
Assets Inventory (1,000 – 800)	200	Capital	5,000
Receivables	1,200	Profit (250 + 1,200 – 800)	650
Cash	5,250		
	6,650		
Liabilities Payables	(1,000)		
	5,650		5,650

(f) **Paid rent**

	£		£
Assets Inventory	200	Capital	5,000
Receivables	1,200	Profit (650 – 250)	400
Cash (5,250 – 250)	5,000		
	6,400		
Liabilities Payables	(1,000)		
	5,400		5,400

(g) **Drawings**

	£		£
Assets Inventory	200	Capital	5,000
Receivables	1,200	Profit	400
Cash (5,000 – 100)	4,900		
	6,300	Drawings	(100)
Liabilities Payables	(1,000)		
	5,300		5,300

(h) **Sundry income**

	£		£
Assets Inventory	200	Capital	5,000
Receivables(1,200+50)	1,250	Profit (400 + 50)	450
Cash	4,900		
	6,350	Drawings	(100)
Liabilities Payables	(1,000)		
	5,350		5,350

(i)   Payment to payable

		£		£
Assets	Inventory	200	Capital	5,000
	Receivables	1,250	Profit	450
	Cash (4,900 – 500)	4,400		
		5,850	Drawings	(100)
Liabilities	Payables(1,000–500)	(500)		
		5,350		5,350

(j)   Receipt from receivable

		£		£
Assets	Inventory	200	Capital	5,000
	Receivables(1,250-1,200)	50	Profit	450
	Cash (4,400 + 1,200)	5,600		
		5,850	Drawings	(100)
Liabilities	Payables	(500)		
		5,350		5,350

(k)   Purchase of van

		£		£
Assets	Van	4,000	Capital	5,000
	Inventory	200	Profit	450
	Receivables	50		
	Cash (5,600 – 4,000)	1,600		5,450
			Drawings	(100)
		5,850		
Liabilities	Payables	(500)		
		5,350		5,350

(l)   Telephone bill

		£		£
Assets	Van	4,000	Capital	5,000
	Inventory	200	Profit (450 – 150)	300
	Receivables	50		
	Cash	1,600		5,300
			Drawings	(100)
		5,850		
Liabilities	Payables (500 + 150)	(650)		
		5,200		5,200

4 Ledger accounting

Workbook Activity 5

Bank

		£			£
(a)	Capital	4,000	(b)	Computer	1,000
(d)	Sales	800	(c)	Rent	400

Capital

	£			£
		(a)	Bank	4,000

Rent

		£		£
(c)	Bank	400		

Sales

	£			£
		(d)	Bank	800

Computers

		£		£
(b)	Bank	1,000		

Workbook Activity 6

Capital

		£			£
			(a)	Bank	4,000

Purchases

		£			£
(b)	Bank	700			
(g)	Bank	1,200			

Entertainment

		£			£
(c)	Bank	300			

Computers

		£			£
(d)	Bank	3,000			

Sales

		£			£
			(e)	Bank	1,500

Drawings

		£			£
(f)	Bank	500			

Telephone

		£			£
(h)	Bank	600	(i)	Bank	200

Stationery

		£		£
(j)	Bank	157		

Bank

		£			£
(a)	Capital	4,000	(b)	Purchases	700
(e)	Sales	1,500	(c)	Entertainment	300
(i)	Telephone	200	(d)	Computers	3,000
			(f)	Drawings	500
			(g)	Purchases	1,200
			(h)	Telephone	600
			(j)	Stationery	157

Workbook Activity 7

Sales

	£		£
		B	1,000
		C	90

Receivable B

	£		£
Sales	1,000	Bank	500

Receivable C

	£		£
Sales	90	Bank	90

Bank

	£		£
Receivable B	500		
Receivable C	90		

Workbook Activity 8

Bank

	£		£
Capital	10,000	Computer	1,000
Sales	2,000	Telephone	567
Sales	3,000	Rent	1,500
Sales	2,000	Rates	125
		Stationery	247
		Petrol	49
		Purchases	2,500
		Drawings	500
		Petrol	42
Sub-total	17,000	Sub-total	6,530
		Balance c/d	10,470
	17,000		17,000
Balance b/d	10,470		

Workbook Activity 9

Bank

	£		£
Capital	5,000	Purchases	850
Sales	1,000	Fixtures	560
Sales	876	Van	1,500
Rent rebate	560	Rent	1,300
Sales	1,370	Rates	360
		Telephone	220
		Stationery	120
		Petrol	48
		Car repairs	167
Sub-total	8,806	Sub-total	5,125
		Balance c/d	3,681
	8,806		8,806
Balance b/d	3,681		

Workbook Activity 10

Bank

	£		£
Balance b/d	23,700	Drawings	4,000
Sales	2,300	Rent	570
Sales	1,700	Purchases	6,000
Receivables	4,700	Rates	500
		Salaries	3,600
		Car expenses	460
		Petrol	49
		Petrol	38
		Electricity	210
		Stationery	89
Sub-total	32,400	Sub-total	15,516
		Balance c/d	16,884
	32,400		32,400
Balance b/d	16,884		

Workbook Activity 11

Trial balance at 31 August 20X9

	Dr £	Cr £
Sales		41,770
Purchases	34,680	
Receivables	6,790	
Payables		5,650
General expenses	12,760	
Loan		10,000
Plant and machinery at cost	5,000	
Motor van at cost	6,000	
Drawings	2,000	
Rent and rates	6,700	
Insurance	4,000	
Bank overdraft		510
Capital		20,000
	77,930	77,930

Workbook Activity 12

Purchases

		£			£
(a)	Payables	1,000			
(j)	Bank	400	Balance c/d		1,400
		1,400			1,400
	Balance b/d	1,400			

Payables

		£			£
(g)	Bank	300	(a)	Purchases	1,000
	Balance c/d	700			
		1,000			1,000
				Balance b/d	700

Rent

		£		£
(b)	Bank	500	Balance c/d	500
		500		500
	Balance b/d	500		

Sales

		£			£
			(c)	Receivables	1,500
	Balance c/d	3,500	(k)	Bank	2,000
		3,500			3,500
				Balance b/d	3,500

Receivables

		£				£
(c)	Sales	1,500	(f)	Bank		400
				Balance c/d		1,100
		1,500				1,500
	Balance b/d	1,100				

Computers

		£			£
(d)	Bank	900	Balance c/d		900
		900			900
	Balance b/d	900			

Wages

		£			£
(e)	Bank	1,000	Balance c/d		1,000
		1,000			1,000
	Balance b/d	1,000			

Telephone

		£				£
(h)	Bank	200	(i)	Bank		50
				Balance c/d		150
		200				200
	Balance b/d	150				

Bank

		£			£
(f)	Receivables	400	(b) Rent		500
(i)	Telephone	50	(d) Computer		900
(k)	Sales	2,000	(e) Wages		1,000
			(g) Payables		300
			(h) Telephone		200
			(j) Purchases		400
Balance c/d		850			
		———			———
		3,300			3,300
		———			———
			Balance b/d		850

Trial balance as at 31 July 20X9:

	Dr £	Cr £
Purchases	1,400	
Payables		700
Rent	500	
Sales		3,500
Receivables	1,100	
Computers	900	
Wages	1,000	
Telephone	150	
Bank overdraft		850
	———	———
	5,050	5,050
	———	———

5 Accounting for credit sales, VAT and discounts

Workbook Activity 2

(a) VAT = £140.00 × 20% = £28.00

(b) VAT = £560.00 × 20% = £112.00

(c) VAT = £720.00 × $\frac{20}{120}$ = £120.00

(d) VAT = £960.00 × $\frac{20}{120}$ = £160.00

Workbook Activity 3

(a) VAT = £(280 – (2% × 280)) × 20% = £54.88

(b) VAT = £(480 – (3% × 480)) × 20% = £93.12

(c) VAT = £(800 – (5% × 800)) × 20% = £152.00

(d) VAT = £(650 – (4% × 650)) × 20% = £124.80

Workbook Activity 4

(a) **B takes the settlement discount:**

	£
Net price	600.00
VAT £(600 – (3% × 600)) × 20%	116.40
Invoice value	716.40

Amount paid by B:

	£
Invoice value	716.40
Less: 3% × 600	(18.00)
Amount paid	698.40

(b) **B does not take the settlement discount:**

	£
Net price	600.00
VAT £(600 – (3% × 600)) × 20%	116.40
Invoice value	716.40

If B does not take the settlement discount, B will pay the full £716.40.

6 Accounting for credit purchases, VAT and discounts

Workbook Activity 1

(a)	VAT = £400 × 20%	=	£80.00
(b)	VAT = £650 × 20%	=	£130.00
(c)	VAT = £528 × $\frac{20}{120}$	=	£88.00
(d)	VAT = £120 × $\frac{20}{120}$	=	£20.00

Workbook Activity 2

(a)	VAT =£(850 – (3% × 850)) × 20%	=	£164.90
(b)	VAT =£(600 – (5% × 600)) × 20%	=	£114.00
(c)	VAT =£(325 – (2% × 325)) × 20%	=	£63.70
(d)	VAT =£(57 – (4% × 57)) × 20%	=	£10.94

Workbook Activity 3

Calculate the invoice value and amount paid by Z.

	£
Net price	600.00
VAT £(600 – (3% × 600)) × 20%	116.40
	———
Invoice value	716.40
Less: Discount 3% × 600	(18.00)
	———
Amount paid	698.40
	———

Purchases

	£		£
Payables	600.00		

Payables

	£			£
Bank	698.40	Purchases + VAT		716.40
Discount	18.00			
	———			———
	716.40			716.40
	———			———

Bank

	£		£
		Payables	698.40

VAT

	£		£
PLCA	116.40		

Discounts received

	£		£
		Payables	18.00

7 Control accounts and subsidiary ledgers

Workbook Activity 5

Sales day book

Date	Invoice no	Customer name	Code	Total £	VAT £	01 £	02 £	03 £	04 £
18/4/X1	06116	B Z S Music		1,455.72	236.52		432.00		787.20
18/4/X1	06117	M T Retail		642.00	107.00	210.00			325.00
18/4/X1	06118	Harmer & Co		1,037.58	168.58		575.00	294.00	
				3,135.30	512.10	210.00	1,007.00	294.00	1,112.20

Note that when a trade discount has been deducted on the invoice in total it must be deducted from each type of sale when entering the figures in the analysed sales day book.

Workbook Activity 6

Sales day book

Date	Invoice no	Customer name	Code	Total £	VAT £	Maintenance £	Decorating £
01/5/X1	07891	Portman & Co	P2	166.24	27.24	139.00	
03/5/X1	07892	Stanton Assocs	S3	1,315.60	215.60		1,100.00
05/5/X1	07893	Boreham Bros	B7	283.20	47.20	106.00	130.00
				1,765.04	290.04	245.00	1,230.00

Workbook Activity 7

			Purchases day book					
Date	Invoice no	Code	Supplier	Total	VAT	Fabric	Header tape	Other
07/4/X1	06738	PL03	Fabric Supplies Ltd	1,120.17	183.57	798.00	138.60	
07/4/X1	0328	PL04	Lillian Fisher	110.04	18.34			91.70
07/4/X1	CN0477	PL05	Headstream & Co	(81.60)	(13.60)	(51.40)	(16.60)	
08/4/X1	07359	PL01	Mainstream Fabrics	336.97	55.45	281.52		
				1,485.58	243.76	1,028.12	122.00	91.70

Workbook Activity 8

			Purchases day book					
Date	Invoice no	Code	Supplier	Total	VAT	Wood	Bricks/ Cement	Consum-ables
1/5/X1	077401	PL16	Magnum Supplies	504.23	82.63		421.60	
1/5/X1	046193	PL08	JR Ryan & Co	120.99	20.16	85.08		15.75
1/5/X1	47823	PL13	HT Todd Plc	442.73	71.93	284.80	86.00	
				1,067.95	174.72	369.88	507.60	15.75

Workbook Activity 9

			Purchases returns day book					
Date	Credit note no	Code	Supplier	Total	VAT	Wood	Bricks/ Cement	Consum-ables
28/4/X1	CN06113	PL13	HT Todd Plc	30.69	4.98	25.71		
28/4/X1	06132	PL03	BL Lukey Ltd	42.57	6.97	35.60		
30/4/X1	C4163	PL16	Magnum Supplies	46.76	7.66		39.10	
				120.02	19.61	61.31	39.10	–

8 Payments and receipts

Workbook Activity 10

FARMHOUSE PICKLES LTD

To: Grant & Co

225 School Lane
Weymouth
Dorset
WE36 5NR
Tel: 0261 480444
Fax: 0261 480555
Date: 30 April 20X1

STATEMENT

Date	Transaction	Debit £	Credit £	Balance £
1 April	Opening balance			337.69
4 April	Inv 32656	150.58		488.27
12 April	Credit 0335		38.70	449.57
18 April	Inv 32671	179.52		629.09
20 April	Payment		330.94	298.15
20 April	Discount		6.75	291.40
24 April	Credit 0346		17.65	273.75
25 April	Inv 32689	94.36		368.11

May we remind you that our credit terms are 30 days

FARMHOUSE PICKLES LTD

To: Mitchell Partners

225 School Lane
Weymouth
Dorset
WE36 5NR
Tel: 0261 480444
Fax: 0261 480555
Date: 30 April 20X1

STATEMENT

Date	Transaction	Debit £	Credit £	Balance £
1 April	Opening balance			180.46
7 April	Inv 32662	441.57		622.03
12 April	Credit 0344		66.89	555.14
20 April	Inv 32669	274.57		829.71
21 April	Payment		613.58	216.13
21 April	Discount		8.45	207.68

May we remind you that our credit terms are 30 days

Workbook Activity 11

Ryan's Toy Shop LTD
125 Finchley Way Bristol BS1 4PL Tel: 01272 200299

STATEMENT OF ACCOUNT

Customer name Arnold's Toys Ltd
Customer address 14 High Street, Bristol, BS2 5FL

Statement date 1st December		Amount		Balance	
Date	Transaction	£	p	£	p
19/11	Invoice 2195	118	08	118	08
20/11	Invoice 2198	2,201	95	2,320	03
20/11	Credit note 2198	323	60	1,996	43
22/11	Cheque	118	08	1,878	35
				1,878	35

Workbook Activity 12

The following problems exist on the cheques received:

Cheque from K T Lopez – not signed

Cheque from L Garry – post dated

Cheque from L Barrett – made out to wrong name

Cheque from P Ibbott – more than six months old

Cheque from J Lovell – discrepancy between words and figures.

Workbook Activity 13

Cheque from BZS Music – settlement discount of £8.64 has been taken – this is valid.

Cheque from Musicolor Ltd – settlement discount of £22.00 has been taken – but is not valid as the cheque has been received after 5 days from the invoice date. However, in the interest of good customer relations, perhaps the discount should be granted but the customer should be informed and reminded of the settlement discount terms.

Cheque from Harmer & Co – settlement discount of £8.82 has been taken – this is valid.

Cheque from Newford Music – settlement discount of £23.76 has been taken – this is not valid as the receipt is too late to claim the discount. Again the discount might be granted in the interest of good customer relations but the customer should be informed and reminded of the settlement discount terms.

Cheque from Trent Music – settlement discount of £13.27 has been taken – however it should have been £11.34 (3% × £378.00). Customer should be informed of the error.

Workbook Activity 14

Step 1

Write up the sales day book.

SALES DAY BOOK

Date	Customer	Total £	VAT £	Sales £
	A	952.00	152.00	800.00
	B	3,808.00	608.00	3,200.00
		4,760.00	760.00	4,000.00

Step 2

Write up the cash receipts book.

CASH RECEIPTS BOOK

Date	Narrative	Total £	VAT £	SLCA £	Cash sales £	Discount allowed £
	A (W)	912.00		912.00		40.00
	B	2,000.00		2,000.00		
	C	360.00	60.00		300.00	
		3,272.00	60.00	2,912.00	300.00	40.00

Working:

Cash paid by A:

	£
Sale value net of VAT	800
VAT	152
	952
Less: Settlement discount (800 × 5%)	(40)
	912

Step 3

Post the totals to the general ledger.

Sales				VAT			
	£		£		£		£
		SDB	4,000.00			SDB	760.00
		CRB	300.00			CRB	60.00

SLCA				Discount allowed			
	£		£		£		£
SDB	4,760.00	CRB	2,912.00	SDB	40.00		
		CRB	40.00				

Step 4

Post individual amounts for the SDB and CRB to the sales ledger.

A				B			
	£		£		£		£
SDB	952.00	CRB	912.00	SDB	3,808.00		2,000.00
		CRB	40.00				

Workbook Activity 15

The entries in the sales ledger will be:

Account name	Amount £	Dr ✓	Cr ✓
McCaul & Partners	147.56		✓
McCaul & Partners	2.95		✓
P Martin	264.08		✓
F Little	167.45		✓
D Raine	265.89		✓
D Raine	7.97		✓

Show what the entries in the general ledger will be:

Account name	Amount £	Dr ✓	Cr ✓
Discounts allowed	10.92	✓	
Sales ledger control account	10.92		✓
Sales ledger control account	844.98		✓

Workbook Activity 16

REMITTANCE ADVICE

To:

Building Contract Supplies
Unit 15 Royal Estate
Manchester
M13 2EF

Nethan Builders
Brecon House
Stamford House
Manchester
M16 4PL

Tel: 0161 521 6411
Fax: 0161 530 6412
VAT reg: 471 3860 42
Date: 18 May 20X1

Date	Invoice no	Amount £	Discount taken £	Paid £
18 May 20X1	07742	203.66	2.55	201.11

Total paid	£201.11
Cheque no	200550

REMITTANCE ADVICE

To:

Jenson Ltd
30 Longfield Park
Kingsway
M45 2TP

Nethan Builders
Brecon House
Stamford House
Manchester
M16 4PL

Tel: 0161 521 6411
Fax: 0161 530 6412
VAT reg: 471 3860 42
Date: 18 May 20X1

Date	Invoice no	Amount £	Discount taken £	Paid £
18 May 20X1	47811	184.21		184.21

Total paid	£184.21
Cheque no	200551

REMITTANCE ADVICE

To:

Magnum Supplies
140/150 Park Estate
Manchester
M20 6EG

Nethan Builders
Brecon House
Stamford House
Manchester
M16 4PL

Tel: 0161 521 6411
Fax: 0161 530 6412
VAT reg: 471 3860 42
Date: 18 May 20X1

Date	Invoice no	Amount £	Discount taken £	Paid £
18 May 20X1	077422	756.35	12.65	743.70

Total paid	£743.70
Cheque no	200552

REMITTANCE ADVICE

To:

Haddow Bros
The White House
Standing Way
Manchester M13 6FH

Nethan Builders
Brecon House
Stamford House
Manchester
M16 4PL

Tel:	0161 521 6411
Fax:	0161 530 6412
VAT reg:	471 3860 42
Date:	18 May 20X1

Date	Invoice no	Amount £	Discount taken £	Paid £
18 May 20X1	G33940	510.93	8.54	502.39

Total paid	£502.39
Cheque no	200553

Workbook Activity 17

The entries in the general ledger will be:

Account name	Amount £	Dr ✓	Cr ✓
Postage	26.25	✓	
Staff Welfare	31.40	✓	
Stationery	19.40	✓	
Travel Expenses	33.01	✓	
VAT	9.12	✓	

Workbook Activity 18

Postage

	£		£
Balance b/d	231.67		
PCB	20.01		

Staff welfare

	£		£
Balance b/d	334.78		
PCB	4.68		

Stationery

	£		£
Balance b/d	53.36		
PCB	12.03		

Travel expenses

	£		£
Balance b/d	579.03		
PCB	20.17		

VAT account

	£		£
PCB	4.94	Balance b/d	967.44

Workbook Activity 19

Voucher total

	£
02634	13.73
02635	8.91
02636	10.57
02637	3.21
02638	11.30
02639	14.66
	62.38

Cash total

		£
£10 note	1	10.00
£5 note	2	10.00
£2 coin	3	6.00
£1 coin	7	7.00
50p coin	5	2.50
20p coin	4	0.80
10p coin	1	0.10
5p coin	2	0.10
2p coin	3	0.06
1p coin	6	0.06
		————
		36.62
		————

Reconciliation of cash and vouchers at 22 May 20X1

	£
Voucher total	62.38
Cash total	36.62
	————
	99.00
	————

The reconciliation shows that there is £1 missing. More cash has been paid out of the petty cash box than is supported by the petty cash vouchers. This could be due to a number of reasons:

- A petty cash claim was made out for, say, £11.30 but mistakenly the amount given to the employee was £12.30.

- An employee borrowed £1 from the petty cash box for business expenses and this has not been recorded on a petty cash voucher.

- £1 has been stolen from the petty cash box.

MOCK ASSESSMENT

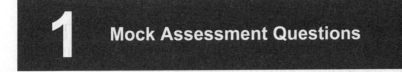

Mock Assessment Questions

Each task is independent.

You must complete all tasks.

Task 1.1

The following transactions all took place on 31 December 20X1 and have been entered into the sales day book as shown below. No entries have yet been made into the ledger system.

Date 20X1	Details	Invoice no.	Total £	VAT £	Net £
31 Dec	Worker Ltd	61612	3,600	600	3,000
31 Dec	P T Associates	61613	720	120	600
31 Dec	Paul Bros	61614	1,200	200	1,000
31 Dec	S D Partners	61615	600	100	500
	Totals		6,120	1,020	5,100

(a) What will be the entries in the sales ledger?

Select your account name from the following list: Paul Bros, PT Associates, Purchases, Purchases ledger control, Purchases returns, Sales, Sales ledger control, Sales returns, S D Partners, VAT, Worker Ltd

Account name	Amount £	Debit ✓	Credit ✓

(b)   What will be the entries in the general ledger?

Select your account name from the following list: Paul Bros, PT Associates, Purchases, Purchases ledger control, Purchases returns, Sales, Sales ledger control, Sales returns, S D Partners, VAT, Worker Ltd.

Account name	Amount £	Debit ✓	Credit ✓

Task 1.2

The following credit transactions all took place on 31 December and have been entered into the **purchases returns day-book** as shown below. No entries have yet been made in the ledgers.

Date 20X1	Details	Credit note number	Total £	VAT £	Net £
31 Dec	L Jameson	318	1,200	200	1,000
31 Dec	K Davison	459	1,080	180	900
	Totals		2,280	380	1,900

(a)   What will be the entries in the purchases ledger?

Select your account names from the following list: K Davison, L Jameson, Purchases, Purchases ledger control, Purchases returns, Sales, Sales ledger control, Sales returns, VAT.

Account name	Amount £	Debit ✓	Credit ✓

(b) What will be the entries in the general ledger?

Select your account names from the following list: K Davison, L Jameson, Purchases, Purchases ledger control, Purchases returns, Sales, Sales ledger control, Sales returns, VAT.

Account name	Amount £	Debit ✓	Credit ✓

Task 1.3

There are five payments to be entered in Adams & Son's cash-book.

Receipts

Received cash with thanks for goods bought. From Adams & Son, a customer without a credit account. Net £400 VAT £80 Total £480 *Johnson Ltd*	Received cash with thanks for goods bought. From Adams & Son, a customer without a credit account. Net £320 VAT £64 Total £384 *A Alpha*	Received cash with thanks for goods bought. From Adams & Son, a customer without a credit account. Net £350 (No VAT) *Bond's*

Cheque book counterfoils

ABC Ltd (Purchase ledger account ABC006) £2,000 (**Note:** Have taken £20 settlement discount) 000123	Twilight (Purchase ledger account TWI001) £240 000124

(a) Enter the details from the three receipts and two cheque book stubs into the credit side of the cash-book shown below and total each column.

Cash-book – credit side

Details	Discount	Cash	Bank	VAT	Payables	Cash purchases
Balance b/f						
Johnson Ltd						
A Alpha						
Bond's						
ABC Ltd						
Twilight						
Total						

There are two cheques from credit customers to be entered in Adam & Son's cash book:

Rhoda Ring   £560 (this customer has taken a £40 discount)

Reef   £210

(b) Enter the above details into the debit side of the cash-book and total each column.

Cash book – debit side

Details	Discount	Cash	Bank	Receivables
Balance b/f		1,500	11,710	
Rhoda Ring				
Reef				
Total				

(c)   Using your answers to (a) and (b) above, calculate the cash balance.

£

(d)   Using your answers to (a) and (b) above, calculate the bank balance.

£

(e)   Will the bank balance calculated in (d) above be a debit or credit balance?

Debit   /   Credit

Task 1.4

The following transactions all took place on 31 December and have been entered in the debit side of the cash-book as shown below. No entries have yet been made in the ledgers.

Date 20X1	Details	Discounts £	Bank £
31 Dec	Balance b/f		3,110
31 Dec	Paul Bros	10	500

(a)   What will be the entries in the sales ledger?

Select your account name from the following list: Balance b/f, Bank, Discounts allowed, Discounts received, Paul Bros, Purchases ledger control, Sales ledger control.

Account name	Amount £	Debit ✓	Credit ✓

(b) What will be the entries in the general ledger?

Select your account name from the following list: Balance b/f, Bank, Discounts allowed, Discounts received, Paul Bros, Purchases ledger control, Sales ledger control.

Account name	Amount £	Debit ✓	Credit ✓

The following transactions all took place on 31 December and have been entered in the credit side of the cash-book as shown below. No entries have yet been made in the ledgers.

Cash-book – Credit side

Date 20X1	Details	VAT £	Bank £
31 Dec	Office expenses	30	180
31 Dec	Travel		48

(c) What will be the entries in the general ledger?

General ledger

Account name	Amount £	Debit ✓	Credit ✓

Select your account name from the following list: Bank, Entertainment, Insurance, Office expenses, Purchases ledger control, Sales ledger control, VAT, Travel.

Task 1.5

The business maintains a petty cash book as both a book of prime entry and part of the double entry accounting system. The following transactions all took place on 31 December and have been entered in the petty cash-book as shown below. No entries have yet been made in the general ledger.

Petty cash-book

Date 20X1	Details	Amount £	Date 20X1	Details	Amount £	VAT £	Travel £	Entertain-ment £	Office sundries £
31 Dec	Balance b/f	100.00	31 Dec	Entertain-ment	9.60	1.60		8.00	
31 Dec	Bank	150.00	31 Dec	Office sundries	12.00	2.00			10.00
			31 Dec	Office sundries	14.40	2.40			12.00
			31 Dec	Travel	10.00		10.00		
			31 Dec	Balance c/d	204.00				
		250.00			250.00	6.00	10.00	8.00	22.00

What will be the FIVE entries in the general ledger?

General ledger

Account name	Amount £	Debit ✓	Credit ✓

Select your account name from the following list: Balance b/f, Balance c/d, Bank, Entertainment, Office sundries, Petty cash-book, VAT, Travel.

Task 1.6

Below is a list of balances to be transferred to the trial balance as at 31 December. Place the figures in the debit or credit column, as appropriate, and total each column.

Account name	Amount £	Debit £	Credit £
Motor vehicles	30,927		
Inventory	28,814		
Bank	10,222		
Petty cash control	200		
Sales ledger control	172,696		
Purchases ledger control	75,987		
VAT owed to tax authorities	63,252		
Capital	28,352		
Loan from bank	17,421		
Sales revenue	646,818		
Sales returns	135,629		
Purchases	273,937		
Purchases returns	1,348		
Discount received	1,700		
Discount allowed	2,340		
Wages	152,099		
Motor expenses	2,853		
Office sundries	5,450		
Rent and rates	7,345		
Advertising	1,452		
Hotel expenses	1,034		
Telephone	599		
Subscriptions	152		
Miscellaneous expenses	9,129		
Totals			

Task 1.7

Earl & Robinson, code all purchase invoices with a supplier code AND a general ledger code. A selection of the codes used is given below.

Supplier	Supplier Account Code
Alpha Ltd	ALP21
Burton Products	BUR14
Cuddington Couriers	CUD22
Farrah Ltd	FAR13
Jacob Brothers	JAC17

Item	General ledger Code
Pasta	GL12
Tomatoes	GL14
Herbs	GL21
Cheese	GL23
Wine	GL34

This is an invoice received from a supplier.

Jacob Brothers
Jacob Brothers **19 Clough Road, Sale M34 5HY** **VAT Registration No. 349 2354 13**

Earl & Robinson

42 Maple Street   20 March 20X2

Audenshaw, M11 2SQ

500 ....Tins of tomatoes @ £0.15 each   £75

VAT   £15

Total   £90

(a)   Select which codes would be used to code this invoice.

Supplier account code	Select your account code from the following list: ALP21, BUR14, CUD22, FAR13, JAC17, GL12, GL14, GL21, GL23, GL34
General ledger code	Select your account code from the following list: ALP21, BUR14, CUD22, FAR13, JAC17, GL12, GL14, GL21, GL23, GL34

Shown below is a statement of account received from a credit supplier, Spence & Co and the supplier's account as shown in the purchases ledger of Alfie Electricals.

Spence & Co

42 Armour Lane, Kilwinning, KA16 7YH

To: Alfie Electricals

1 Albert Street

Edinburgh, EH1 4BH

STATEMENT OF ACCOUNT

Date 20X2	Invoice Number	Details	Invoice Amount £	Cheque Amount £	Balance £
1 Oct	232	Goods	900		900
5 Nov	248	Goods	400		1,300
6 Nov	269	Goods	300		1,600
23 Nov	–	Cheque		900	700
26 Nov	299	Goods	100		800

Spence & Co

Date 20X2	Details	Amount £	Date 20X2	Details	Amount £
23 Nov	Bank	900	1 Oct	Purchases	900
26 Nov	Bank	700	5 Nov	Purchases	400
			6 Nov	Purchases	300

(b) Which item is missing from the statement of account from Spence & Co?

[   ]

Select your account name from the following list: Invoice 232, Invoice 248, Invoice 269, Invoice 299, Cheque for £700, Cheque for £900

(c) Which item is missing from the supplier account in Alfie Electricals purchases ledger?

[   ]

Select your account name from the following list: Invoice 232, Invoice 248, Invoice 269, Invoice 299, Cheque for £700, Cheque for £900

(d) Assuming any differences between the statement of account from Spence & Co and the supplier account in Alfie Electricals purchases ledger are simply due to omission errors, what is the amount owing to Spence & Co?

£ [   ]

Task 1.8

Alfie Electricals sends BACS remittance advice notes to suppliers on the last day of the month following the month of invoice. Alfie Electricals' bank is Tandanda and Robison Wholesale banks with Bank of Money. Below is an uncompleted BACS remittance advice and an extract from Alfie Electricals' purchases ledger.

Alfie Electricals

1 Albert Street

Edinburgh, EH1 4BH

BACS REMITTANCE ADVICE

To:

Date:

The following payment will reach your bank account within 3 working days.

Invoice number	Credit note number	Amount £
Total amount paid		

Robison Wholesale

Date 20X2	Details	Amount £	Date 20X2	Details	Amount £
18 May	Purchases returns credit note CN119	543	17 May	Purchases Invoice 318	5,430
26 May	Purchases returns credit note CN138	250	21 June	Purchases Invoice 350	1,798
30 June	Bank	4,637	28 June	Purchases Invoice 382	987
			7 July	Purchases Invoice 400	1,402

(a) To whom will the BACS remittance advice be addressed? (Select one)

Tandanda   Alfie Electricals   Robison Wholesale   Bank of Money

(b) What will be the date shown on the BACS remittance advice? (Select one)

31 May   30 June   31 July   15 August

(c) What will be the TWO items shown on the BACS remittance advice?

	✓
Purchase invoice number 318	
Purchase invoice number 350	
Purchase invoice number 382	
Purchase invoice number 400	
Purchase credit note number CN119	
Purchase credit note number CN138	

(d) What will be the total amount paid?

£ [   ]

(e) Which of the following statements is true? (Select one)

The BACS remittance advice informs the customer of the amount payable to Tandanda.

The BACS remittance advice informs the supplier of the amount payable by Bank of Money.

The BACS remittance advice informs the customer of how much will be paid into its bank.

The BACS remittance advice informs the supplier of how much will be paid into its bank.

On 1 December Alfie Electricals delivered the following goods to a credit customer, Erin Electric.

Alfie Electricals

1 Albert Street

Edinburgh, EH1 4BH

Delivery note No. 189

01 Dec 20X2

Erin Electric   Customer account code: ER01

Walker Way

Middlesborough

10 amplifiers, product code AMP999.

The list price of the goods was £500 per amplifier plus VAT (20%). Erin Electric are to be given a 5% trade discount and a 3% early settlement discount is offered if paid within 5 days.

(f)   Complete the invoice below.

Alfie Electricals

1 Albert Street

Edinburgh, EH1 4BH

VAT Registration No. 299 1728 12

Erin Electrics   Customer account code:

Walker Way   Delivery note number:

Middlesborough

                                             Date: 1 Dec 20X2

Invoice No: 950

Quantity of amplifiers	Product code	Total list price £	Net amount after discount £	VAT £	Gross £

Alfie Electricals is offered a certain discount by a supplier, dependent on whether the amount due is settled within a certain timescale.

(g)   What is the name of this type of discount?

[   ]

Select your account name from the following list: Bulk discount, Settlement discount, Trade discount

Task 1.9

The following is a summary of transactions with Crompton's, a new credit customer.

£500 re invoice 189 of 11 Dec
£600 re invoice 201 of 19 Dec
£350 re credit note 129 of 20 Dec
£980 re invoice 234 of 23 Dec
Cheque for £1,100 received 24 Dec

Complete the statement of account below.

<table>
<tr><td colspan="4" align="center">Alfie Electricals
1 Albert Street
Edinburgh, EH1 4BH</td></tr>
<tr><td colspan="2">To: Crompton's</td><td colspan="2" align="right">Date: 31 Dec 20X2</td></tr>
<tr><td>Date 20XX</td><td>Details</td><td>Transaction amount £</td><td>Outstanding amount £</td></tr>
<tr><td></td><td></td><td></td><td></td></tr>
<tr><td></td><td></td><td></td><td></td></tr>
<tr><td></td><td></td><td></td><td></td></tr>
<tr><td></td><td></td><td></td><td></td></tr>
<tr><td></td><td></td><td></td><td></td></tr>
</table>

Task 1.10

It is important to understand the difference between capital expenditure, revenue expenditure, capital income and revenue income.

(a) Select one option in each instance below to show whether the item will be capital expenditure, revenue expenditure, capital income or revenue income.

Item	Capital expenditure	Revenue expenditure	Capital income	Revenue income
Purchase of stationery				
Receipts from cash sales				
Receipt from sale of machinery				
Purchase of additional machinery				
Payment of rates				
Receipts from credit sales				

(b) Show whether the following statements are true or false.

A receivable is someone who is owed money by the business.

True   False

If the owner invests cash into the business, the capital balance increases.

True   False

A credit increases an item of income.

True   False

(c) Classify each of the following items as an asset or a liability.

Item	Asset or liability?
Bank loan	Select Asset OR Liability
Motor vehicle	Select Asset OR Liability
Money due from customers	Select Asset OR Liability

Mock Assessment Answers

Task 1.1

(a)

Account name	Amount £	Debit ✓	Credit ✓
Worker Ltd	3,600	✓	
P T Associates	720	✓	
Paul Bros	1,200	✓	
S D Partners	600	✓	

(b)

Account name	Amount £	Debit ✓	Credit ✓
Sales ledger control	6,120	✓	
VAT	1,020		✓
Sales	5,100		✓

Task 1.2

(a)

Account name	Amount £	Debit ✓	Credit ✓
L Jameson	1,200	✓	
K Davison	1,080	✓	

(b)

Account name	Amount £	Debit ✓	Credit ✓
Purchases ledger control	2,280	✓	
Purchases returns	1,900		✓
VAT	380		✓

Task 1.3

(a) **Cash-book – credit side**

Details	Discount	Cash	Bank	VAT	Payables	Cash purchases
Balance b/f						
Johnson Ltd		480		80		400
A Alpha		384		64		320
Bond's		350		–		350
ABC Ltd	20		2,000		2,000	
Twilight			240		240	
Total	20	1,214	2,240	144	2,240	1,070

(b) **Cash book – debit side**

Details	Discount	Cash	Bank	Receivables
Balance b/f .		1,500	11,710	
Rhoda Ring	40		560	560
Reef			210	210
Total	40	1,500	12,480	770

(c) £286

(d) £10,240

(e) Debit

Task 1.4

(a)

Account name	Amount £	Debit ✓	Credit ✓
Paul Bros	500		✓
Paul Bros	10		✓

(b)

Account name	Amount £	Debit ✓	Credit ✓
Discounts allowed	10	✓	
Sales ledger control	500		✓
Sales ledger control	10		✓

(c)

Account name	Amount £	Debit ✓	Credit ✓
Office expenses	150	✓	
VAT	30	✓	
Travel	48	✓	

Task 1.5

Account name	Amount £	Debit ✓	Credit ✓
VAT	6.00	✓	
Travel	10.00	✓	
Entertainment	8.00	✓	
Office sundries	22.00	✓	
Bank	150.00		✓

Task 1.6

Account name	Amount £	Debit £	Credit £
Motor vehicles	30,927	30,927	
Inventory	28,814	28,814	
Bank	10,222	10,222	
Petty cash control	200	200	
Sales ledger control	172,696	172,696	
Purchases ledger control	75,987		75,987
VAT owing to tax authorities	63,252		63,252
Capital	28,352		28,352
Loan from bank	17,421		17,421
Sales revenue	646,818		646,818
Sales returns	135,629	135,629	
Purchases	273,937	273,937	
Purchases returns	1,348		1,348
Discount received	1,700		1,700
Discount allowed	2,340	2,340	
Wages	152,099	152,099	
Motor expenses	2,853	2,853	
Office sundries	5,450	5,450	
Rent and rates	7,345	7,345	
Advertising	1,452	1,452	
Hotel expenses	1,034	1,034	
Telephone	599	599	
Subscriptions	152	152	
Miscellaneous expenses	9,129	9,129	
Totals		834,878	834,878

Task 1.7

(a) Supplier account code – JAC 17

General ledger code – GL14

(b) Which item is missing from the statement of account from Spence & Co?

Cheque for £700

(c) Which item is missing from the supplier account in Alfie Electricals purchases ledger?

Invoice 299

(d) Assuming any differences between the statement of account from Spence & Co and the supplier account in Alfie Electricals purchases ledger are simply due to omission errors, what is the amount owing to Spence & Co?

£100

Task 1.8

(a) Robison Wholesale

(b) 31 July

(c)

Purchase invoice number 318	
Purchase invoice number 350	✓
Purchase invoice number 382	✓
Purchase invoice number 400	
Purchase credit note number CN119	
Purchase credit note number CN138	

(d) What will be the total amount paid?

£2,785

(e) The BACS remittance advice informs the supplier of how much will be paid into its bank,

(f)

	Alfie Electricals
	1 Albert Street
	Edinburgh, EH1 4BH

VAT Registration No. 299 1728 12

Erin Electrics   Customer account code: ER01

Walker Way   Delivery note number: 189

Middlesborough

Date: 1 Dec 20X2

Invoice No: 950

Quantity of amplifiers	Product code	Total list price £	Net amount after discount £	VAT £	Gross £
10	AMP999	5,000	4,750	921.50	5,671.50

(g)

Settlement discount

Task 1.9

	Alfie Electricals		
	1 Albert Street		
	Edinburgh, EH1 4BH		
To: Crompton's			Date: 31 Dec 20X2

Date 20XX	Details	Transaction amount £	Outstanding amount £
11 Dec	Invoice 189	500	500
19 Dec	Invoice 201	600	1,100
20 Dec	Credit note 129	350	750
23 Dec	Invoice 234	980	1,730
24 Dec	Cheque	1,100	630

Task 1.10

(a)

Item	Capital expenditure	Revenue expenditure	Capital income	Revenue income
Purchase of stationery		✓		
Receipts from cash sales				✓
Receipt from sale of machinery			✓	
Purchase of additional machinery	✓			
Payment of rates		✓		
Receipts from credit sales				✓

(b) *A receivable is someone who is owed money by the business.*

False

If the owner invests cash into the business, the capital balance increases.

True

A credit increases an item of income.

True

(c)

Item	Asset or liability?
Bank loan	Liability
Motor vehicle	Asset
Money due from customers	Asset

INDEX